WHAT'S MY
TWEEN
THINKING?

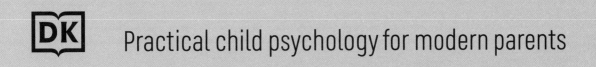

Practical child psychology for modern parents

WHAT'S MY **TWEEN** THINKING?

Tanith Carey

Clinical Psychologist
Dr Angharad Rudkin

Foreword by
Carl Pickhardt

CONTENTS

CHAPTER 1

Your 8–10-year-old

CHAPTER 2

Your 10–12-year-old

FOREWORD

One common challenge that many parents have with their preteen child is ignorance about how adolescence typically unfolds. They may not know what common changes to anticipate, as growing up predictably alters the child, the parent in response, and the relationship between them.

Many parents could use assistance understanding how this coming-of-age transformation commonly proceeds. With this book, good help is here. For each section, there is:
- A telling adolescent statement or question the child might be saying or asking
- A scenario description: defining the growth issue of concern
- An explanation of what the adolescent might be thinking
- An explanation of what the parent might be thinking
- Suggested ways parents can helpfully respond

A great strength of this book is that the author doesn't traffic in generalities. She sticks to specifics. She gets right in there with parents, where they live, in the messy and confusing day-to-day interactions, and then addresses complicated questions: "Why might this be happening?" "What might I helpfully do?" "What might I constructively say?"

The book also addresses specific adolescent changes, including:
- Less physical affection and more privacy with parents
- Social pressures of belonging and conforming with peers
- More risk-taking from increased desire to act impulsively
- Coping with competition to get what one wants in life
- Increased self-consciousness over changes from puberty

You will also find many helpful pieces of parenting advice, my personal favorite being this:

The chairperson of their brain—the prefrontal cortex—is also helping your tween decide what to say out loud, and what to process internally, so they are more likely to be secretive. However, keeping up communication is essential for maintaining a strong connection to your child. The time you invest in keeping the channels of communication open, and being available to answer any questions they have about the world, will pay off many times over in the years to come.

The strength of this book is how it accepts, explains, and advises parents about how raising an adolescent is more complicated than raising a child. The author portrays a great diversity of specific changes that typically mark adolescent development. Taken together, they explain why the hardest half of growing up and the hardest half of parenting often come last.

Parents can use all the understanding they can get. And now this book is here to help them remain connected to their tween as adolescent separation gradually grows them apart, which it is meant to do.

CARL PICKHARDT

Carl Pickhardt

TWEEN
DEVELOPMENT

No longer a child; not yet a teenager—your tween is in a key development period. The coming years will see new challenges, from friendship fallouts to mood swings, which happen before your child is cognitively old enough to understand them.

However, armed with some knowledge of their brain development, you will be able to help them understand how they are changing. While the brain almost reaches adult size by the start of puberty, there is a lot of internal wiring to be done. Over the next few years, axons (long, thin tendrils that stretch between the nerve cells and carry information) will get coated with the fatty substance myelin—like insulation on electrical wires. Known as myelination, this strengthens and speeds up the communication between the brain cells by thousands of times, enabling tweens to integrate both sides of their brains. This allows their thinking to become more sophisticated, while the gradual release of hormones can make them more emotionally reactive. The other big change is that brain cells that are not needed are pruned, enabling tween brains to become more efficient. It is now that your tween starts to specialize and stand out from the crowd, thanks to their talents, qualities, or interests. It's an exciting and rewarding period.

THE EARLY TWEEN YEARS
YOUR 8–10-YEAR-OLD

As your tween moves from early childhood into adolescence, they start to be able see the world in more complex and nuanced ways.

How your tween thinks

◉ Your tween's brain has now reached close to full adult size.

◉ Tween thinking is now more organized and rational. This concrete, black-and-white thinking leads them to believe things are either "right" or "wrong."

◉ If they don't get all the facts, tweens use "magical thinking," which means they make up a story to connect the dots on what they don't yet understand.

◉ Planning is easier now, as their higher-order thinking means they can start to see more clearly and imagine the future.

◉ More adultlike memories are being laid down now that the prefrontal cortex, which governs attention span and planning, is more developed.

◉ Concentration span expands so that by the end of this phase tweens can focus for up to half an hour on new or interesting tasks.

◉ Seeing another point of view is now possible, as your tween's brain—especially the frontal lobes—are now better connected. This allows them to understand that other people have their own thoughts and feelings. They also understand it's possible to have mixed emotions about the same event.

◉ Tweens take rules seriously. They will now protest about what is "fair" and "unfair."

How your tween feels

◉ While younger children are more interested in themselves, tweens start to care a lot about what others think of them and want to fit in more.

◉ As they become more aware of what they need to do to be favorably compared, winning becomes more important.

◉ Your tween will be more private and want to keep secrets, as they realize they can keep their thoughts to themselves and you can't read their minds.

◉ They have become aware that their body is different from yours and others, so they now want to bathe and dress on their own.

◉ Tweens are now more aware of traditional gender roles and expectations and how much they live up to them.

How your tween acts
- Tweens want to test their newfound strength, coordination, and stamina with running races, gym moves, and physical games.
- Play is still an important part of life, but they are moving away from make-believe to more rule-based games.
- Friendship skills expand as children use their knowledge of others' thoughts and feelings to make friends.

- Peers are becoming more important, but they still spend most of their free time with family.
- As competition ramps up, they now care more about who wins and loses.
- Collecting can become a passion—be it hair accessories, stickers, or erasers. Tweens hope to win social acceptance by getting a full set.
- As they figure out how to do better at an activity, they want to show off their skills to peers and parents.

THE LATER TWEEN YEARS
YOUR 10–12-YEAR-OLD

Most of what adults see as challenging behavior in the tween years has both an upside and an evolutionary purpose. It reflects the hormonal shifts and brain remodeling they are going through.

How your tween thinks
- Synaptogenesis—the growth of connections in the brain and pruning of unused brain cells—means that a tween's brain is becoming more specialized and efficient at the skills they are good at and that they practice.
- Your tween may start to think in more abstract, complex ways and form new ideas and opinions. They think more about hypothetical situations and their place in them.
- Tween friendships are getting closer and more meaningful but also more complicated. They are becoming more sensitive to the growing differences between them and are watching each other to see who is showing the first signs of puberty.
- As tweens think more about how their peers will judge them, they start to envisage an "imaginary audience" watching them at all times, even when there are no other peers present. As a result, they become acutely self-conscious.

How your tween feels

- Peer pressure is starting to have a more powerful effect. Because they want to fit in, your tween is more likely to want to conform.
- Within friendship groups, there will now be unwritten rules about how members act, behave, and dress.
- Rising and falling hormones—estrogen and testosterone—will have a knock-on effect on a tween's brain chemistry, making them moodier.
- Rising levels of testosterone in both genders are linked not only to more sexual thoughts but also a drive for social status.
- There is a dip in self-esteem as tweens become more aware of the social world and their standing in it in terms of looks, skills, and academics.

How your tween acts

- Crushes are becoming more likely as tweens get a "dopamine squirt," or rush of pleasure in their brain's reward circuit when they see someone they are attracted to.
- Now they understand double meanings and irony, funny jokes, and word games are popular, and they may test boundaries with humor.
- Being good at something becomes a way of gaining acceptance from peers, whether through schoolwork, sports, music, art, or gaming.
- Tweens start to spend more time with friends and less with family, as they identify their "tribe."
- As they start to value independence, they want more choice about the food they eat, walking on their own, or arranging their social lives.
- As they become more status-orientated, they may ask for certain brands so that they fit in.

HOW WERE YOUR OWN
TWEEN YEARS?

We tend to remember our tween years as the golden era in our childhood. They are so vivid because we see and experience many things for the first time at this stage, and key moments—both happy and sad—will stick with us.

Our tween years were when we discovered our interests, formed our first real friendships, and had the first inklings of our potential before life got a bit more complicated in the teen years. And, if we were fortunate, as we formed our identity in this delicate phase, we had our needs met by our caregivers. We felt physically safe, significant to our families, connected and treasured, able to learn and grow, and free to make some of our own decisions.

Even though our parents probably set out wanting to do their best for us, life often gets in the way. They may have been struggling with their own unmet needs handed down from their parents. They may have been dealing with poverty, divorce, death, addiction, threat, or mental health difficulties. And, unless we give it some conscious thought, we can pass unhelpful patterns down to our children.

If it was obvious to us what was missing in our own tween years, we may try to overcompensate and give our kids what we felt we didn't have, causing us to go too far the other way. On the other hand, we may find ourselves getting irrationally angry when our kids do something we were once shamed for as children. We may not know exactly why; we just know it brings up uncomfortable feelings buried deep within us.

Unpacking such patterns takes work, but with the help of this book, we hope you can stay in the moment, so you can parent the child you have, not the one you used to be.

Becoming self-aware
The first step to parenting in the present, rather than the past, is to notice when you have disproportionately strong feelings about something your tween does. Ask yourself what it is bringing up for you. To help with this, each scenario in this book contains a section called "What you might be thinking." While we can't possibly know everything crossing your mind,

> ## ONE OF THE GREATEST GIFTS YOU CAN GIVE YOUR CHILD IS NOTICING YOUR EMOTIONAL STATE AND REGULATING IT.

see this as an invitation to consider what else is happening for you. What experiences—or unprocessed fear or hurts—from your childhood might be getting in the way of you dealing with this situation in the present?

If your tween has done something understandable at this stage in their development, yet it sparks rage, irritation, disgust, jealousy, or resentment, step away. One of the greatest gifts you can give your child is noticing your emotional state and having the skills to regulate it, especially if it's going to be hurtful to others. Make time to think or talk through what has happened with a co-parent if you have one, or another caring adult, until you can bring your reaction back to the moment.

Being empathic

The second step to parenting in the present is to make a conscious effort to view a challenging situation through your child's eyes, not just through your own. This is why for each scenario we have included a section called "What they might be thinking." This is to ground you in the here and now. Deliberately setting out to understand your tween's perspective will shift you into asking what their behavior is trying to communicate, so you can meet your child where they are now.

WHAT ARE
YOUR FAMILY VALUES?

Bringing up a tween can be challenging: puberty is starting younger than in previous generations; there is competition from screens; and school is more pressurized. As your job is to guide your tween, it may help to consider which values are guiding you.

Values are the beliefs you stand for. They are probably already integral to who you are, but you may not have thought to crystallize them. Now is the time.

The tween years are the period of development when you are at your most influential. During this delicate period of identity formation, your tween has never watched you more carefully to try to figure out how to be in the world. When things get choppy, as they inevitably will, having a family mission statement to refer to can be the firm anchor for both you and them.

Tweens feel more secure and grounded when they get clarity and direction because it gives them a better idea of what is expected of them. When challenges come up, they will have a compass to guide them.

What matters most to you?
Now that your child has reached the end of early childhood, take a moment before setting off on the next leg. Look at the list of values on the next page with your co-parent, if you have one.

Discuss which values are important to you and which are important to you as a family. See if there are ones you can agree on so you can stay on the same page. When you have thought about them, talk about them with your tween and say why you feel they are important. It will help them understand why you make the parenting choices you do.

If your tween has some values they'd like to add, maybe they could draw them as a family coat of arms to keep on the fridge as a reminder of what's important.

For each of the following questions, pick out one or two values from the list below that are most important to you:

- What is important to you as a parent?
- What kind of parent do you aspire to be?
- What sort of relationship would you like to build with your child?
- How would you behave if you were the ideal version of yourself?
- How would you like to hear people describe your child?
- How would you like your child to describe you later in life?

adventurous **forgiving** loyal **fun** independent
polite **honest** **humorous** patient **kind** creative
balanced cuddly **controlled** compassionate
friendly self-aware **trustworthy** mindful
empathetic upstanding **affectionate** **reliable**
confident flexible **strong**

CHAPTER 1

YOUR
8 – 10
YEAR-OLD

"DON'T DO THAT, MOM!"

Your child has always been happy to hold your hand and be affectionate in public, and it may have become something you take for granted. So the first time they pull away from your touch, it can be surprising and hurtful.

SCENARIO | You go to hold your tween's hand at the school gate and they pull away from you, saying, "Don't do that, Mom!"

From the moment your child was born, you were the center of their world. As they relied on you for their survival, they grew up thinking you could do no wrong. However, now your tween is starting to pride themselves on being more independent and developing an "imaginary audience" to help them fit in with their peer group. This means they are constantly anticipating what other children think about them, even when no one's watching. In the moment, your tween's fear of looking babyish is greater than the comfort they get from holding your hand.

WHAT YOU MIGHT BE THINKING

You may feel sad that the child who could once never get enough of you is now moving into a phase where they no longer seem to need you as much.

WHAT THEY MIGHT BE THINKING

⦿ **Part of learning independence is practicing how it feels** not to be attached all the time. Your tween may now see holding your hand as "babyish."

⦿ **A boy may pull back quicker from his mom now** that he identifies less with her gender and feels he must be more like his dad.

⦿ **Tweens are in an egocentric phase of thinking** and are still learning empathy. As your child views you as an omnipotent grown-up, they may not realize they have the power to hurt your feelings.

⦿ **Your child may feel physically uncomfortable.** Brain scans show that young people suffer more acute symptoms of stress than adults if they feel they are being watched or judged.

HOW YOU COULD RESPOND

In the moment

Respect their wishes
Now that your child is becoming self-conscious, agree to treat them in a more grown-up way when you both appear in front of others.

Don't take it personally
This is more about your child's development than about you. Their words are a sign they trust you to keep loving them, no matter what they say.

In the long term

Give perspective
To let your child know you understand, at another moment, talk about when you were their age and felt embarrassed by your parents, through no fault of theirs.

Talk about communication
One of the roles of parents is to help kids understand others' feelings. At a neutral time, ask your tween to consider how their words might be received by others. Practice helping them to communicate their needs in kinder ways.

Keep being affectionate
For most children, physical affection is still a key way to be soothed. Even though your tween may not want to be seen holding your hand in public, they are still likely to need physical connection at home. Stroke their back for reassurance or ask them if they would like a hug. Look for other ways to connect, such as playing new games or showing an interest in their hobbies.

Brace yourself
Come to terms with the fact that for the next few years, your tween will often find you embarrassing, whatever you do. Look forward to a future when your grown-up child has a stronger sense of self and is happy to show their love for you in public again.

SEE RELATED TOPICS
That's babyish: pp.98–99
Don't tell me what to do: pp.118–119

❝ ❞

TALK ABOUT WHEN YOU WERE THEIR AGE AND FELT EMBARRASSED BY YOUR PARENTS.

"ARE WE **THERE YET?**"

When you're on a long trip, it can be frustrating if your bored tween repeatedly asks: "Are we there yet?" and never seems satisfied with the answer. It may help you to know there are good reasons why they ask this question.

SCENARIO | Your tween keeps asking: "Are we there yet?" on a road trip and you are beginning to lose patience.

Your tween is still developing their understanding of time and distance, and still learning how to delay gratification. Time is a difficult, abstract concept to grasp and partly depends on an "internal clock," which develops as children improve their memories and attention spans. Research has also found that time passes more slowly for children because it takes up a bigger proportion of their lives. Tweens are also still building their tolerance to uncertainty and their ability to entertain themselves when they feel bored, so traveling long distances can feel interminable.

WHAT YOU MIGHT BE THINKING

You may feel frustrated that your tween is never satisfied, no matter how many times you give an update. You may think they are old enough to know better.

SEE RELATED TOPICS
I've got nothing to do: pp.60–61
I just can't sit still: pp.68–69

WHAT THEY MIGHT BE THINKING

⊙ **Tweens are used to structured days**. Being stuck in the car with no say over what happens next means they may seek information and reassurance. They expect adults to know the answers.

⊙ **They may feel irritated by being restrained.** Kids this age are physically stronger and nap less than when they were little. In the US, they must use a car or booster seat until they are 4ft 9in tall, or about 8 to 12 years old.

⊙ **If they are staring at gadgets in a moving vehicle**, they may feel carsick. If screens are their default entertainment, they may not know how to make time pass without them.

⊙ **Uncomfortable experiences feel longer to children** than to adults, studies have found—probably because they have no control over when it will end. So, a two-hour trip could feel longer to your child than it does to you.

HOW YOU COULD RESPOND

In the moment

Acknowledge their feelings
Help your tween put their frustration into words and summarize it so they know you understand. Be empathic by acknowledging that you also feel constrained buckled up with a seat belt, but it's a law to keep everyone safe.

Give praise
Notice when they entertain themselves. When kids are quiet on trips, parents often say nothing, hoping the peace lasts. Instead, praise your tween for being patient and entertaining themselves so they learn this is what they are expected to do.

Share updates
Help them track the trip. Instead of using hours and minutes, use markers they can relate to more easily, such as, "We'll be there after lunch," or "when it gets dark." Show them visually on a map or GPS, or give them a compass so they can chart your progress.

In the long term

Focus on the fun
While they don't need the constant chatter that toddlers do, tweens still benefit from entertainment and conversation. To make the trip go faster, play interactive games with the whole family, such as podcast quizzes, through the car stereo.

Help them visualize
Research shows that the brain can't tell the difference between real and imagined experiences. Talk about what you're looking forward to doing once you get there.

Track the time
Have fun with their time-telling skills. If your tween has an analogue watch, ask them to tell you the next time the big hand gets to the 12. If they have a digital watch, get them to set an alarm every hour to mark another passing, then start a new game on the hour so they have something to look forward to.

"I'LL BE **HOMESICK**"

When they were little, your child was primed to want to stay close to you. But even though separation is an inevitable part of growing up, some tweens will need more support to spend longer periods of time away from you.

SCENARIO | Your tween is worried about their upcoming class trip. They say they will be too homesick spending a night away from you.

You are the person who makes your tween feel safest, and home is the center of their world, where everything feels known. How your child reacts to being separated from you, as they begin to become more independent, will depend on how sensitive they are to change, as well as genetic and environmental factors. Research has shown that 10 to 12 percent of children come into the world with a slightly more vigilant nervous system, which makes them more cautious in new situations. However, learning to manage fear of the unknown and cope with uncomfortable feelings is an important life skill.

WHAT YOU MIGHT BE THINKING

Your tween's separation anxiety could be standing in the way of them experiencing new things and their classmates will think they are "babyish."

❝ ❞

YOU COULD PACK A TRANSITIONAL OBJECT—A SMALL NIGHTLIGHT OR A KEEPSAKE.

WHAT THEY MIGHT BE THINKING

◉ **They may have picked up the idea that they can't cope** for long periods without you, especially if health issues, or your anxieties, have made you protective.

◉ **An unfamiliar environment might make them worry** about everyday things like going to the bathroom and sleeping in the dark—made worse by you not being nearby to soothe them.

◉ **They may compare themself to classmates** and feel ashamed they don't feel brave enough to spend a night away from home.

◉ **Other signs of separation anxiety may show,** such as not wanting to sleep alone and worrying about what will happen to you when they are away.

HOW YOU COULD RESPOND

In the moment

Listen
Even if you feel panicked that your child is refusing to go on the trip, ask them to name their worries so they can process them.

Normalize their feelings
Tell them feeling homesick is a natural response to being away from familiar places. Knowing nearly everyone experiences it can ease their fears. Talk about how it comes in waves and is likely to disperse when they get involved in activities on the trip.

Have a brainstorming session
Ask your tween what might help them feel less homesick. You could pack a transitional object—a small nightlight or a keepsake.

Empower them
Suggest they use brave talk, telling themself in a kind, firm tone, "You can do this." This will encourage them to work through their fears. Remind them of other times they have been away without you, such as staying overnight with grandparents.

In the long term

Check your own anxiety
Children have a finely tuned radar for your feelings. If you found it hard to leave them at school, stayed with them at parties, or had "elastic band farewells," where you kept checking on them, they may have picked up that they are not safe without you. Manage your own anxiety first.

Build social muscles
Practice regular short separations. Try a "half sleepover" at a

friend's house, collecting them at 9 p.m., building up to overnight.

Help them stick it out
If your tween has a phone, it can be tempting to check in. Studies show that staying in touch too much makes homesickness worse. Don't offer to pick them up early as they won't learn to tolerate uncomfortable feelings.

Practice confident partings
Whether it's a quick hug or a fist pump, a confident goodbye will assure them they can manage.

SEE RELATED TOPICS

I don't want to go to Grandma's: pp.96–97
I don't want to go to school: pp.108–109

COMMUNICATING
WITH TWEENS

Your tween may no longer be the little chatterbox they once were. Now that their thinking is becoming more complex, they begin to realize that they can keep more of their thoughts to themself.

The chairperson of their brain—the prefrontal cortex—is also helping your tween decide what to say out loud, and what to process internally, so they are more likely to be secretive. However, keeping up communication is essential for maintaining a strong connection with your child. The time you invest in keeping these channels of communication open, and being available to answer any questions they have about the world, will pay off many times over in the years to come.

1

Timing is everything
Look for signs that your tween wants to talk—they may hang around, drop hints about issues, and ask for help finding things at bedtime. Accept these as hints they may want to chat.

4

Let them off-load
Your child has to contain their behavior all day, so may come home and download a litany of complaints. This enables them to process their feelings and move on. If in doubt, ask: "Do you want my help, or do you just want to vent?"

“ ”

SPEND REGULAR
TIME TOGETHER
DOING THINGS
YOUR TWEEN
LIKES TO DO.

WORKING THINGS OUT

8 key principles

2

Build an emotional vocabulary
If your tween is struggling to express their feelings, help them summarize what they are telling you to show that you are listening. By learning to name their emotions, they will be better able to manage them.

3

Use a two-way diary
Leave a two-way diary by a child's bed, in which they can ask questions and talk about their feelings, and you can write answers and loving messages. This can really aid communication. If they don't like writing, suggest they draw how they feel.

5

Avoid offering quick fixes
When your tween opens up about a problem, it is natural to want to fix it. Offering immediate solutions will make them feel their worries are trivial, their distress is not being heard, and you want their problems to go away. Aim to be a comforting presence, traveling alongside them.

6

Have one-on-one time
Spend regular, unhurried time together, doing things your tween likes to do. Put a hold on any criticism or judgment and show delight in spending time with them. Making these "emotional deposits" shows your child you like the person they are becoming and will make it easier to communicate at other times.

7

Ask about their friends
Tweens may reveal more about their thoughts and feelings when they talk about what their friends are doing and saying. Try other "side doors," such as watching movies together or chatting about current events to help them talk about how they see the world.

8

Validate their feelings
Even if your tween's emotions are uncomfortable to hear, make the effort to understand. This helps them listen to, trust, and manage feelings. Often an acknowledgment is all that's needed. It's often what you don't say that makes you the best sounding board and helps your child feel safe and heard.

!

TAILORED ADVICE

8–10
YEARS OLD

Share their interests
Tweens often love compiling lists of facts. Even if you've heard the same fact 100 times, be curious, and ready to say: "Tell me more."

Watch your criticism
Even if it's done out of love, tweens can often hear our suggestions as criticism, which can make them close down. Help them feel safe around you by looking for opportunities to compliment, such as, "I love your curiosity" or "You have a great sense of humor."

10–12
YEARS OLD

Use tech
If your tween has a phone, set up a family WhatsApp group to send supportive texts or funny GIFs. This reminds your tween that you love and think about them when you are not with them.

Be a trusted source
As they want more privacy, your tween may get concerned that you will tell people, perhaps including the parents of their friends. Let them know that it is safe to confide in you and that you won't tell others.

"I WANT A **DOG**"

Children grow up seeing images of animals in picture books and movies—and friends may have pets too. Now that your child is at an age where they feel more responsible, they may ask for a real-life animal companion.

SCENARIO | After stroking a dog in the park, your tween becomes very persistent in asking whether they can get one.

Just as they were once nurtured, tweens now feel competent enough to give love and protection to another living being. At a time when they feel more judged and compared in the classroom hierarchy, a pet can fulfill an important role for children in this age group; a furry friend will feel like a noncritical ally who belongs to them, is always there to listen, looks up to them, and makes them feel good about themselves. Research has found that a loved and cared-for companion animal can help tweens in a range of ways, from reducing stress, screen time, and loneliness to increasing empathy.

WHAT YOU MIGHT BE THINKING

You may wonder if your tween is ready for the responsibility and work that looking after a dog brings, and whether you will end up looking after it instead.

SEE RELATED TOPICS
All my friends have a phone: pp.62–63
I don't need a babysitter: pp.190–191

WHAT THEY MIGHT BE THINKING

⊚ **Most tweens are not mature enough to understand** how much work it takes to look after another living being. Even so, your tween may repeatedly insist that none of the care will ever fall to you.

⊚ **As tweens learn they don't have to disclose everything** to adults, they may look forward to having an animal confidant who they can pour out all their secrets to and who will never tell anyone.

⊚ **They will love to cuddle a pet** without realizing it raises the levels of the feel-good chemical oxytocin and reduces the stress hormone cortisol, calming them.

⊚ **Owning a pet will form part of their developing identity,** helping them feel more powerful and in control, and offering new ways to play more grown-up roles. Dogs in particular can feel like animal versions of younger siblings but without the rivalry.

IF DAILY TASKS ARE STILL A CHALLENGE, THEY MAY NOT BE READY TO LOOK AFTER PETS.

HOW YOU COULD RESPOND

In the moment

Be curious
Ask your tween why they want a pet. You could say, "I know it looks fun to have a dog, but there are a lot of jobs that come with it. Can you think what they are?"

Get them thinking
Your tween may easily be emotionally swayed by a pet's cuteness and the idea of having something to cuddle. While you say you understand this, ask them to use their logic, too, and list pros and cons for the whole family.

Make sure it's not a phase
Look for ongoing signs that your child is not just in love with the idea of having a dog. Gauge their level of interest and commitment. Are they researching breeds? Are they thinking about the practicalities, such as feeding and toilet habits? Do they have empathy for animals and can they anticipate their needs? If you're not sure, offer to dogsit for a friend so you can see how they respond.

In the long term

Can your tween look after themself?
Do they brush their teeth and pack their school bag without being asked? If you have to nag them to do daily tasks, they aren't ready to take sole responsibility for a pet.

Decide as a family
Bringing a companion animal into your home can't be one child's decision. Consider the cost, your property, and how much you are at home to care for the pet.

Accept your role
Your tween should have an active role in caring for a pet, but they are unlikely to be ready to be solely responsible. Accept that caring for an animal will fall to everyone.

Teach empathy
Read animal behavior books together, so your tween understands that pets feel fear, like humans. This will make them less likely to bully them.

"RACE YOU THERE!"

During the tween years, you may notice your child is more competitive. As they become stronger and more coordinated, they may want to test their developing physical skills against each other whenever they get the chance.

SCENARIO | As you take your child and two friends home for a playdate, they turn the final stretch home into a race that your tween is determined to win.

Tweens are honing many of their physical skills, such as running, jumping, climbing, and skipping. They are also getting more muscular, and because of their light frames and quicker reaction times, running can feel particularly exhilarating for them. It is normal for them to compare themselves to their peers and to jostle for positions in hierarchies as they try to make their mark. To prove they are top dog, they may turn every physical activity into a competition, especially if they think they have a chance of winning. As proud as you may be of your child's achievements, help them see how trying to beat others all the time can potentially damage friendships. Role model and talk about being a gracious winner.

WHAT YOU MIGHT BE THINKING

You may wonder why your tween turns everything into a contest and be concerned it will annoy others. However, you may also see this competitive spirit as something positive that will set them up well for life.

WHAT THEY MIGHT BE THINKING

⊚ **Your tween wants to be master of the world**—they're likely to make sure you know their latest achievements by giving you constant bulletins.

⊚ **They are now feeling eager to show off the skills** that prove they can look after themself without adult help.

⊚ **Your tween is comparing themself more to their peers** and will know exactly where they rank in different skills, both sporting and academic.

⊚ **"Showing off" may peak at this stage**—in the later teen years, they start to see their achievements in a more realistic context once they realize their peers view this behavior as "bragging" and bigheadedness."

" "

SUGGEST THAT THERE IS ONLY ONE PERSON IN LIFE WHO IS TRULY WORTH BEATING, AND THAT'S THEMSELF.

HOW YOU COULD RESPOND

In the moment

Acknowledge their energy
There's no need to big-up your child further if they win the race, but acknowledge how good it is to see them being active. Now that your tween has proved they are the fastest runner, you could also suggest other activities to the group that are less competitive and involve more teamwork, such as building a fort.

In the long term

Encourage personal bests
At neutral times, you could suggest to your child that there is only one person in life who is truly worth beating, and that's themself. If they see how far they have come, they will also see how far they can go. Make it clear that for them to succeed, others don't have to fail.

Acknowledge others' strengths
Explain that everyone has a special strength or skill. Tell your child while they may be good at running, their friends may be very good at math or drawing.

Don't impose your expectations
If you often push your child, because it makes you feel good as a parent, they may feel they need to win at everything to get your approval. Avoid compliments based on comparisons, or praising your child by putting others down.

Encourage teamwork
Kids who are raised with a cooperative approach to their peers are likely to be more emotionally resilient, creative, and open-minded. If your child has a dominant personality, you could channel them into activities where leadership and collaboration are encouraged, such as Scouts or Brownies.

Look for special skills
If your child feels like they are often the loser in running or sports, they can internalize this as "failing." Help them discover other activities that could suit them better, perhaps martial arts, chess, or music.

SEE RELATED TOPICS
They say I'm a show-off: pp.58–59
I got the best grade: pp.88–89

"I DON'T WANT A BATH TONIGHT"

Now that your child is older, bathtime won't have the same appeal.
A reluctance to have a bath or shower unfortunately coincides
with hormonal changes and an increase in body odor that
makes personal hygiene even more important.

SCENARIO | You notice your tween is starting to develop body odor,
but they still insist they don't need a bath.

At around the age of eight or nine, the first sign of puberty is when the body's two to four million sweat glands become more active. Although the fluid is odorless, when decomposed by bacteria, it causes a musty smell. However, because humans quickly get acclimatized to new aromas to avoid sensory overload, your tween may not be aware of the smell or realize they need to wash regularly. This also comes at a time when tweens no longer want you to bathe them—they may be noticing how their bodies are changing and may want to keep these changes to themselves.

WHAT YOU MIGHT BE THINKING

You may be worried about how to tell your tween that they have body odor without making them feel angry, hurt, or embarrassed, but equally want to ensure they don't get teased about it.

SEE RELATED TOPICS
I'm old enough to stay up late!: pp.42–43
It's not gross; it's funny!: pp.80–81

WHAT THEY MIGHT BE THINKING

◉ **They may hear your reminders to wash as an interruption** to other fun things they would like to do more, especially if they now have less downtime due to increasing homework.

◉ **Your tween may enjoy being in charge of their body** now that they are older and resent any interference from you.

◉ **They may think you are imagining it** or implying there is something wrong with their body, as they can't smell their sweat as strongly as you can.

◉ **Your tween may associate bathtime with babyish activities**, especially if they have younger siblings who still take part in this routine regularly.

" "

TELL THEM HAVING GOOD SELF-CARE SENDS THE MESSAGE THAT THEY RESPECT THEMSELF.

HOW YOU COULD RESPOND

In the moment

Be direct
Say in a warm, matter-of-fact way: "I love you, and it smells to me like you're a bit sweaty. It's just your body doing its job and developing the odors we all get when we grow up. It's also a sign that you need to wash your body every day now."

Give the bigger picture
Explain that puberty will be a time of very gradual growth caused by hormones over the next few years. Make it clear you are always available to answer any questions.

Suggest showers
Rather than having a time-consuming bath, show tweens how they can get their bodies clean in a few minutes in the shower if they wash under their arms.

In the long term

Make it nonnegotiable
While parents have flexibility on some issues, hygiene is not one of them. Help your child build showering into their routine, the same as brushing teeth. If they need an extra prompt, the single word "shower" will soon become enough to remind them.

Help them be more aware
While tweens may not have smelled their own sweat, they may have noticed classmates' body odor. Explain that having good self-care also sends out an important message that they like and respect themself.

Make being clean fun
Talk about how a shower can be a great way to reset or unwind after a long day. Take them on a shopping trip to smell different shower gels and deodorants so they can choose their favorites and enjoy the experience.

VIDEO GAMING

Many tweens are now moving from make-believe games in the real world to playing them on a screen. They are also moving toward Formal Operational Thinking so are more interested in logic, reasoning, and rules.

Well-designed video games appeal to the natural developmental shifts at this age, as well as offering the illusion of unlimited power in a virtual world, full of color, action, and instant gratification. For boys, video gaming can be like the equivalent of social media for girls—a way to connect—as well as a chance to compare skills. Video games help tweens of all genders develop strategy and teamwork and are a safe outlet for taking risks. However, look for signs that they are playing to the exclusion of other activities, such as schoolwork or spending time with peers in the real world. If your tween says they don't want to do those things, it may be a sign that they are using video games to avoid social or academic issues they find challenging. It's important to address the underlying difficulty.

1
Mention health
Tell your tween that in the same way they need a healthy diet and enough sleep, they need a good mix of activities to feel well. Help them see their life as a pie chart and to keep an eye on whether video games are taking up too big a slice.

4
Make them self-aware
Explain that video games are designed to hook you in and deliver hits of feel-good chemicals to leave you craving more. Ask them to notice signs of playing too much, such as a racing heart or sweaty palms that linger after the game is finished.

WORKING THINGS OUT

6 key principles

2
Play along
Play the video game with your tween to understand what they get out of it. They will enjoy being the expert. Studies have found that when parents play, they get a more realistic understanding of what gaming is about. Then, tweens are likely to respect your opinion more when it comes to setting limits.

3
Monitor use
Look for signs your tween is overdoing it. This could include being more reactive, refusing to stop playing, struggling to concentrate in less stimulating settings, such as the classroom, and gaming in secret. If you feel there's a cause for concern, connect with your tween to find the reasons.

5
Agree on clear boundaries
Together with your tween and co-parent, if you have one, discuss fair limits. Set family mealtimes so there is a regular, expected end to screen time in the evenings. Keep gaming in common areas of your home and make it clear it's never allowed in the bedroom. Hold the line so the rules become routine.

6
Communicate
Talk regularly about what your child is playing and who with. Do they know everyone on their contacts or friends list? Make it clear that any chat with players they don't know should be only about the game and to tell an adult if they are worried. Reassure them that they won't get in trouble.

> **PLAY THE VIDEO GAME WITH YOUR TWEEN TO UNDERSTAND WHAT THEY GET OUT OF IT.**

! TAILORED ADVICE

8–10
YEARS OLD

Stick to age ratings
There are many creative and challenging games available for this age. Buying violent or sexist games meant for older players may make them think rules don't apply.

Do your research
If you are not sure about a game, check it out on a parent advisory site, such as Common Sense Media.

Use parental controls
Free video games make money out of persuading players to pay for add-ons. Install double authentication so your child cannot spend without your permission.

10–12
YEARS OLD

Talk about language
As they play more mature games, your tween is likely to hear "trash talk" and may join in. If you hear bad language, ask them what they think it means and tell them it's not acceptable in the real world.

Offer fun alternatives
If gaming is your tween's main hobby, explain that while you are happy they love it, at this age it's also good to develop skills for the real world. Suggest outdoor activities such as camping, sailing, or skateboarding.

"IS **SANTA** REAL?"

You want to be a trusted source of information for your child. So when they start to question whether Santa exists, you may wonder how to tell them you haven't been truthful.

SCENARIO | Your tween asks you if Santa is real because their classmates claim that grown-ups fill stockings and buy Christmas presents.

Since Victorian times, parents have delighted in telling young children the tale of how a jolly, bearded man in a red suit climbs down the chimney on Christmas Eve to deliver toys. Many grown-ups use the story as a way to influence a child's behavior by claiming that Santa brings more presents to youngsters who are "nice," not "naughty."

According to research, children's excitement about Santa peaks at around the age of five, but most start doubting his existence at around the age of eight. This coincides with a stage of development when tweens are learning to think more logically and can better understand the difference between fantasy and reality.

WHAT YOU MIGHT BE THINKING

- - - - - - - - - -

You may worry that your child will be disappointed that you've been lying and feel like a magical part of their childhood is coming to an end.

WHAT THEY MIGHT BE THINKING

◉ **Your child is becoming a "concrete operational thinker,"** which means they start to use logical ways of thinking to figure out how the world works. So they are likely to already be questioning how Santa leaves them gifts if they don't have a chimney for him to climb down, or how he reaches every child in the world in one night.

◉ **Children expect grown-ups to tell them the truth,** so it is confusing to hear from older siblings or classmates that their parents have lied. As they trust you the most, they will want you to confirm that the rumors they have heard are true.

◉ **Your tween may be confused** that so many adults, and society as a whole, seem to be complicit in the deception that Santa is a real person.

◉ **Your tween may still be unsure,** so they may actively look for evidence that you are Santa, such as noticing price tags being left on toys.

HOW YOU COULD RESPOND

In the moment

Dial down the myth
Kids are more likely to feel angry if they feel manipulated. Avoid using Santa to influence behavior by threatening that he won't bring them gifts if they're naughty.

Help them work it out
If your tween wants to know if Santa is real, ask them what they think and why. If they are asking, it's a sign that they are ready to know the truth. As they draw their own conclusions, support their findings and answer their questions honestly.

Reassure yourself
Research has found that children who have a rich fantasy life are better able to tell the difference between fact and fiction. Now that your child is older, they are also likely to view knowing the truth about Santa as a sign they are more grown-up and "in the know," instead of being angry with you for deceiving them.

In the long term

Help them spread the joy
Once they've figured it out, say that you pretended to be Santa to make their Christmas more magical. Show them they can do the same by giving surprise gifts to others, like buying a Secret Santa for a friend. Explain that it's still fun for younger siblings, and they can be one of your elves.

Explain the meaning of Santa
Your tween is now ready to view Santa as an abstract concept, who sums up the essence of the Christmas spirit in the same way that the Easter Bunny is a symbol of rebirth in spring. You could also give more historical context by explaining that Santa Claus is based on Saint Nicholas, a third-century Turkish bishop who was famous for his kindness. Explain that his generosity sets a good example. Praise them for their detective work, and don't let them feel embarrassed for believing in Santa for so long.

SEE RELATED TOPICS
I'm a superhero: pp.38–39
Are you going to die too?: pp.78–79

" "

IF THEY ARE ASKING, IT'S A SIGN THAT THEY ARE READY TO KNOW THE TRUTH.

"JUST **ONE MORE** GAME"

For many tweens, there are few activities more important to them, and their friendships, than video gaming. Even so, it's essential for them to find a healthy balance between online and real-world interactions.

SCENARIO | Your tween reacts angrily when asked to stop playing their video game and wants to play one more game.

Multiplayer video games give tweens a sense of belonging, and being good at them can help them win social status among peers. Gaming can encourage strategy and problem-solving skills. The constant challenges and bright, realistic graphics can make video games feel more rewarding than real-world activities. While studies have found that playing video games for an hour a day can be good for psychological well-being, playing for more than three hours is linked to antisocial behavior, irritability, and poorer grades. From the outset, help your tween balance how much time they spend in the offline and online worlds.

WHAT YOU MIGHT BE THINKING

You may be worried about how gaming affects your child's behavior and think it is isolating your child from the rest of the family.

WHAT THEY MIGHT BE THINKING

⊙ **Your tween feels competent**, powerful, and in command of their world when they are gaming. They get to call the shots, so it's tough for them to transition back to a place where adults tell them what to do.

⊙ **If your tween plays multiplayer games**, the other players are likely to be an important part of their social life and they will not want to let them down.

⊙ **They could be in the most vital part of the game**, so telling your tween abruptly to get off their console may frustrate them.

⊙ **Your tween feels they deserve downtime after school**, and see playing video games as just that. They may struggle to find anything more immediately rewarding to do with their time.

“ ”

TALK ABOUT HOW, JUST AS WE ALL NEED A VARIED DIET AND ENOUGH SLEEP, WE NEED A MIX OF ACTIVITIES TOO.

HOW YOU COULD RESPOND

In the moment

Let them finish
Recognize that it's hard for your tween to move on immediately from something so absorbing. Agree that they can finish at the end of the next game, which gives a natural pause.

Give good reasons
Rather than just saying, "You've been playing that game for two hours," explain why you want them to stop now, whether it's so they can eat a proper meal, spend some time with family, or get ready for bed. This helps them learn to prioritize other things alongside gaming.

Help them transition
Give your tween time to pivot and reset their brains. You can help by offering them a grounding sensory experience, like a drink of cold juice, to bring their awareness back to the real world.

In the long term

Discuss boundaries
Schedule gaming after important activities. Discuss fair boundaries for starting and finishing, like no gaming until after homework. Set family mealtimes so there is an end to screen time each day. Hold the line so the rules become routine.

Help them notice time passing
Kids lose track of time. If you allow an hour of gaming, set a timer for 45 minutes to give a 15-minute warning before it's time to finish.

Suggest screen-free days
Limit your tween to a few set weekdays, with days off in between. Look at their usage across the week, as they may want to play more on weekends. Keep consoles in common areas so you can monitor time spent on them.

Promote a healthy mix
Rather than being against games, be for other activities. Talk about how, just as we all need a varied diet and enough sleep, we need a mix of activities too.

Encourage self-awareness
Explain that gaming is designed to be addictive. Suggest they look for signs of overuse, like feeling hyped-up afterward. Play along: your tween is more likely to listen if you have shared the experience.

◀ **SEE RELATED TOPICS** ▶
All my friends have a phone: pp.62–63
I didn't think you'd mind: pp.74–75

"I'M A **SUPERHERO!**"

The world can feel like a scary place in which tweens have little control over what happens. Pretending to be a superhero gives them the chance to role-play being fearless and having unlimited power.

SCENARIO | Your tween is running around the house in a mask and cloak, shouting: "I'm going to save the world!"

In early childhood, boys and girls play in similar ways and show interest in the same toys. As they grow up, boys tend to be more drawn toward pretending to be superheroes. One possible reason is that due to higher levels of testosterone, boys are more eager to test their physical strength by climbing, running, and chasing, which are all rolled into superhero games. These tendencies can be reinforced by messages they get from the world about how boys "should" always be fearless, strong, and dominant. With guidance, both boys and girls can feel able to play these empowering roles.

WHAT YOU MIGHT BE THINKING

If you have a son, you may be wondering if playing a superhero is encouraging him to play a hypersexualized masculine role.

SEE RELATED TOPICS
Race you there!: pp.28–29
They say I'm a show-off: pp.58–59

WHAT THEY MIGHT BE THINKING

◉ **Your tween is learning about concepts of goodness** and fairness by swapping between playing the roles of both goodies and baddies with friends.

◉ **Being a hero and having enemies to defeat** gives your tween a chance to show how clever and powerful they can be, and gives them a safe outlet for any angry feelings they may have.

◉ **By taking on this character, they are practicing being brave** and proactive in other scary situations, such as when they are being teased or bullied.

◉ **Your tween son may have observed** that superheroes never show any feelings other than anger and a need for revenge—and they may confuse this with what it means to be "a real man," unless given other messages.

HOW YOU COULD RESPOND

In the moment

Be supportive
Superhero games are a great outlet for tweens of all genders to play together to develop an understanding of right and wrong—as long as the role-play is balanced and kids take turns playing goodies and baddies.

Set boundaries
When playing superheroes with others, suggest that your tween thinks about simple rules, like suspending the game if other participants say "stop," aren't smiling, or start to cry.

Keep it safe
Suggest that whenever they want to play this game, your tween first checks that they are playing in a wide-open space where they won't get hurt. Encourage them to play superheroes outside as much as possible, to allow them to test their physical limits.

In the long term

Keep it gender neutral
Avoid showing more interest or complimenting your son for playing traditional masculine roles. Support mixed-gender playdates and encourage girls to pretend to be all-powerful characters too.

Promote fairness
Ask your tween about their games. Who are they pretending to be and why? Who are they fighting? Talk about how in real life, true heroes come in all genders, are courageous, and do things to help others. They also solve problems with words, rather than with violence.

Think about storybooks
If children read more stories where boys are heroes and girls are invisible or passive, they may internalize these messages. Talk about role models of all genders and in all fields of work, as well as in the circle of people around you.

Empower them
Help your tween meet their need for power and control in other ways. For example, encourage them to help choose what to have for dinner or how they want to decorate their bedrooms. Ask them what superpower they would like to have in real life and why.

> ## ENCOURAGE GIRLS TO PRETEND TO BE ALL-POWERFUL CHARACTERS TOO.

"THEY'RE TEASING ME"

It's upsetting if your tween tells you others are teasing them. However, as long as they are not being deliberately and persistently targeted, all children must learn to cope with some "normal" social pain.

SCENARIO | Your child tells you a classmate is making fun of them by mispronouncing their name to make others laugh.

Although we tend to think of teasing as a precursor to bullying, there are good and bad types. When done affectionately between close friends, particularly boys, good teasing can be playful and affectionate. However, at this age, children are figuring out that they can earn social power by making fun of others, so they may be seeking to test that. If your tween is intentionally and regularly picked on by a socially more powerful classmate in front of others, it may cross the line into bullying, and tweens will need support to stand up to it.

WHAT YOU MIGHT BE THINKING

You may be angry and want to contact the other child's parents. It may also bring up uncomfortable feelings for you if you remember being teased.

WHAT THEY MIGHT BE THINKING

⊙ **Children are forming their identity** based on what their peers think of them at this age, so they can be highly sensitive to name-calling.

⊙ **Teasing can be a test by tweens** to see who is a "crybaby," especially by those who have just been through this phase themselves. If your tween has reacted emotionally before, their peers may tease them to provoke another reaction.

⊙ **Your tween's hurt will be amplified** by the fact that no one watching stood up for them, especially if others laughed. This "bystander effect" will make your child feel humiliated and alone.

❝ ❞

MEAN REMARKS WILL NEVER CUT QUITE AS DEEP IF YOUR CHILD FEELS LOVED AT HOME.

SEE RELATED TOPICS
Nothing's the matter: pp.46–47
They didn't save me a seat at lunchtime: pp.72–73

HOW YOU COULD RESPOND

In the moment

Thank them for telling you
Offer comfort. Cruel words can be as painful as physical blows. Listen more than you speak and help them name how they feel without judging or advising.

Stay calm
Resist the temptation to call the other child's parents. Your tween needs you as their firm anchor, not a bodyguard. If you overreact, they may worry that you will wade in and make it worse.

Don't look for a quick fix
You may be tempted to tell them to laugh it off or tease back, but only your child understands the social dynamic.

Encourage questioning
When they feel less upset, talk through ways they could respond. Suggest that they call out the behavior with questions such as, "Are you okay?" "Can you repeat that?" or "What do you mean?" This will show they aren't an easy target. They could also practice assertiveness, asking to speak to the perpetrator alone, telling them they want the comments to stop. Many will then back down.

In the long term

Give perspective
All children need to learn to deal with "normal social conflict." Labeling every act of meanness as bullying won't help. Bullying is defined as a deliberate, long-term campaign by a more powerful child against a socially weaker one to cause hurt.

Explain teasing
To help your child take mean teasing less personally, explain how it is often done to look powerful at the target's expense.

Support them at home
Help build your child's self-worth by making it clear you like them and want to spend time with them. Mean remarks from others will never cut quite as deep if your child feels loved and supported at home.

Promote a growth mindset
Tweens are prone to black-and-white thinking; they may think that because they are being teased, they will always be a victim. Friendships change fast at this age. Explain that just because someone was mean today, it doesn't mean they won't make it up tomorrow. However, if they often run into friendship issues, help your child practice their social skills and how to improve them.

"I'M OLD ENOUGH
TO STAY UP LATE!"

Even though getting enough sleep is critical for good health, growth, and mood, you may find your tween putting a lot of effort into fighting going to bed, especially now that they see later bedtimes as a status symbol.

SCENARIO | Although clearly tired, your tween insists they are old enough to stay up to watch a TV show their friends are talking about at school.

As they get older, tweens feel entitled to stay up later because they no longer feel "little." If they have younger siblings, they may see later bedtimes as a privilege that proves they are more grown-up.

This is an in-between phase when your child will feel they should have a say about their bedtime. Knowing the effect lack of sleep can have on health, it will be up to you to keep thoughtful limits.

WHAT YOU MIGHT BE THINKING

You might worry about how your child's health and ability to function will be affected, especially when they have to go to school the next day.

WHAT THEY MIGHT BE THINKING

◉ **Your tween sees adults as having ultimate freedom** because they can stay up as long as they like. They may view being sent to bed as being "banished" to somewhere boring. So they may deny it when they are tired.

◉ **Staying up later gives them a chance to spend time with you** on their own without younger siblings, especially if they've been busy with homework and extracurricular activities.

◉ **They may try to negotiate if you've given in before** because you are too tired to enforce bedtimes. They may accuse you of not being fair, which is another way of saying they don't like your decision.

◉ **If you are watching a TV series that is being talked about** at school among their peers, they will be more desperate to stay up so they can sound grown-up to their friends the next day.

◆ SEE RELATED TOPICS ◆
Can I go on a sleepover?: pp.82–83
I'm so tired: pp.160–161

TELL THEM THEIR BODY AND BRAIN NEED REST TO WORK WELL.

HOW YOU COULD RESPOND

In the moment

Show that you understand
Demonstrate that you hear them and understand their disappointment by saying, "I understand you want to stay up later. We'd love that too, but I wouldn't be doing my job as a parent if I let you stay up as long as you like. Your body and brain need rest to work well."

Explain their sleep needs
Talk about sleep as a biological necessity, not a luxury, and how we need varying amounts of sleep at different stages. You could say, "At your age, you need more sleep than grown-ups because your body and brain are growing faster than ours. When you're older, you can stay up later."

Put them to bed
Parents of tweens can overestimate a tween's ability to be independent. Ease the transition by offering to put them to bed with a chat, story, and kiss goodnight. They will look forward to bedtimes as a special time with you.

In the long term

Offer choice
If they are missing out on time with you, work with your tween to reorganize their evenings so that you have more time together. Could they start their homework earlier, or free up time by showering in the morning? Suggesting options will give your tween a sense of control, making them more likely to abide by the bedtimes you set.

Agree on timings
As a rule, tweens need 9 to 12 hours of sleep, so work backward from the time they need to get up. To give flexibility, you could allow a later bedtime on weekends, but keep it to no more than an hour later.

Write down bedtimes
Once bedtimes have been agreed on, write them down and stick them on the fridge. Agree that you will review their bedtime in the years to come, depending on how easy they find it to get up in the mornings.

"I WANT A **HUG**"

As babies, touch was the first and most important form of communication and made your child feel safe. Now that your tween is bigger and more independent, you are likely to have less physical contact, but staying close remains an important way to show them love and acceptance.

SCENARIO | You have had a disagreement with your child. Afterward, when everything has calmed down, they ask you for a hug.

When your child was little, you may have spent most of the day physically close, whether they sat on your lap or were carried. As they grow, the amount you touch can fall away, until a peck on the cheek at bedtime becomes your only physical contact. Invited, affectionate touch never loses its power to reassure. A hug sends a message to the body to release the bonding hormone oxytocin and reduce the stress hormone cortisol. Cuddling is a key way to calm your tween's nervous system and help them bounce back from difficult experiences. If they learn to be soothed by hugs, it will teach them a healthy form of emotional regulation.

WHAT YOU MIGHT BE THINKING

You may wonder whether hugging will send a message that you approve of their behavior. You may also wonder if they are getting too "big" for cuddles.

WHAT THEY MIGHT BE THINKING

● **For a tween who has touch as a "love language"**—or views this as an important form of affection—hugs, kisses, strokes, and hand holding will help reassure them you love them no matter what. Every child will vary in the amount they want to be physically touched.

● **Hugging you may bring back memories** of when they were little and felt safe. It reinforces the message that you are their primary carer and protector.

● **They may want a hug from you to say sorry** and to ask for a signal from you that you can move on and put the conflict behind you. Affectionate touch from you will reinforce the message that you love them more than any verbal praise or gift you can buy them.

● **Although your tween is becoming more independent,** they still need to refuel without being made to feel they are "too big" for this type of affection. They will also need more cuddles when they feel stressed or ill.

SEE RELATED TOPICS
I'll be homesick: pp.22–23
Are you going to die too?: pp.78–79

HOW YOU COULD RESPOND

In the moment

Put away any misgivings
By asking for a hug, your child is asking to reconnect and put the disagreement behind you. Thank them for asking because they recognized this is the best coping mechanism for this moment.

Attach no conditions
Giving your tween a hug when they ask shows that you are also ready to repair your relationship, whatever has been said. Draw a line under what has happened by saying nothing and being present so your child feels safe and loved unconditionally.

Sink into that hug
A range of studies have found that hugs of between 10 and 20 seconds raise oxytocin levels in the body and reduce the levels of the stress hormone cortisol. If your child is asking for a hug, make it last.

In the long term

Give a daily dose
View affection as a way to keep your child emotionally and physically healthy. Loving touch stimulates the areas of the brain associated with social and emotional development. It also lowers the risk of depression, improves immune response, reduces bodily inflammation, and lays the groundwork for satisfying adult romantic relationships. Offer hugs in times of transition, uncertainty, or if your tween is stressed or sad.

Be creative
As well as hugs, look for other ways to communicate your love, such as a fist bump in passing, a reassuring hand squeeze, a hair ruffle, a shoulder massage when they are stressed, or rough-and-tumble play when they have energy. Find out what suits them best and aim for four meaningful touches a day to help them feel loved. Some tweens may want you to show closeness in other ways, such as sitting next to them while they read or watch a movie.

Regulate their feelings
If they look upset or anxious, ask if they would like a hug. However, make sure any hug is being offered to meet their needs, not yours. If they don't want a hug, offer warm words instead.

Teach body autonomy
Tell your tween that in the same way as they asked you for a hug, others should ask for permission to touch them, and they can always say no.

"NOTHING'S THE MATTER"

When they were younger, your child may have had a tantrum when they didn't get what they wanted. Now, in the tween years, they may sulk instead, and if you ask them what's wrong, they are likely to reply with, "Nothing."

SCENARIO | When you tell your tween you won't have time to shop for something they want, they mope around and give you one-word answers.

To your tween, you are still an all-powerful adult. They notice they still have to do what grown-ups tell them most of the time. They have learned that throwing a tantrum is stressful and embarrassing, for them as well as you, and it would be "babyish." By trial and error, or by copying others, they may have started sulking in a nonconfrontational way to resist your authority or express their annoyance. However, it's important to show your tween there are more effective ways to communicate. When children are taught to express their emotions politely, but assertively, they gain a lifelong skill.

WHAT YOU MIGHT BE THINKING

You may be confused about whether to ignore the sulking or tell them to stop. Eventually, you may get frustrated and angry, making it look like you are in the wrong.

SEE RELATED TOPICS
I hate you!: pp.94–95
Nothing! It was just a normal day: pp.116–117

WHAT THEY MIGHT BE THINKING

◉ **Your tween may feel overwhelmed with feelings,** such as frustration, resentment, and anger, but not yet have the words to express this. It feels less risky to refuse to talk or to communicate through body language, such as folding their arms.

◉ **Your tween knows it's difficult to correct them** because they aren't doing anything "wrong." This can briefly make them feel like they have the upper hand, but they may be unsure how to come out of a sulk without losing face.

◉ **If they feel ignored or less important than others** in the family, they may see if withholding affection gets the attention and love they crave.

◉ **They may have got the message growing up** that only "bad" children show anger and that expressing their feelings will be met with disapproval.

HOW YOU COULD RESPOND

In the moment

Have a chat
You may be tempted to ignore the sulking and talk to your tween as normal, but it's important that they learn better ways to communicate. Break the deadlock by offering to help them express their point directly. Show that you'd like to reconnect. In a caring and nonconfrontational way, say something like: "I feel like you are angry and upset with me today. If that is the case, let's talk about the reasons as I'd like to hear how you feel."

Create a fantasy
Give your child in fantasy what you couldn't give them in reality. To show you understand, you could say: "I know you wanted to go to the store and I wish we had been able to, but on this occasion we ran out of time and had to get home. Next time, we can plan our trip differently." Research shows that imagining a positive experience stimulates the brain's reward circuits in the same way as experiencing it in real life.

In the long term

Talk about anger
Explain that anger is a natural response to frustrating life events, which eases when expressed. Encourage them to show their feelings and needs directly and calmly, and explain that others can't read their minds. Don't shame them, so they always feel safe to talk about feelings.

Help them name feelings
Train your child in interoception—helping them notice and name their feelings, including anger, frustration, disappointment, or loss. This allows them to process

them. Studies show that children are better at expressing emotions when they have been shown how to describe them, so name your own feelings, too.

Check your behavior
Avoid passive-aggressive behavior yourself. Research has found that parents who use the silent treatment with their children to express their displeasure are likely to raise children who use the same tactics. Let your tween see you role-model assertive, expressive communication with both them and others.

> **LET YOUR TWEEN SEE YOU ROLE-MODEL ASSERTIVE, EXPRESSIVE COMMUNICATION.**

"KEEP OUT!"

Your tween's bedroom is no longer a place where they just sleep and keep their toys. Now that they are developing a stronger sense of self, their room has become an extension of them and a place where they can go for privacy and to develop their own interests.

SCENARIO | You go to your tween's bedroom to find they have put a sign on the door saying "Keep out!"

Now that your tween is developing their taste in hobbies, movies, music, and collectibles, their room will grow in importance. It's the one space that belongs only to them and is a treasured sanctuary where they can escape, process their feelings, and recharge their batteries. Furthermore, putting up a "Keep out!" sign indicates that your child is deciding what they share with you and what to keep private. Now that their bodies are starting to develop, they may want to get used to these physical changes out of your view. Not all tweens have their own room, so at this stage they may appreciate a privacy screen—a curtain or piece of furniture, like a bookshelf. If there's space, give each child their own storage.

WHAT YOU MIGHT BE THINKING

You may struggle to take this new boundary seriously. Once you realize they mean it, you may feel pushed away and wonder what they are doing. Not knowing everything about your tween is a hard adjustment.

WHAT THEY MIGHT BE THINKING

⊚ **Your child once believed you knew everything they did** and thought. Now they understand that you can't tell what they are thinking. As they break away, they will want some privacy.

⊚ **Tweens are using magical thinking**—a belief that if they think it, it will happen—by putting a "Keep out!" sign on the door. They believe the instruction really will stop you—and siblings—from coming in without permission.

⊚ **If your tween has playdates or sleepovers**, having a room where they spend time with their friends, showcase their interests, such as any collections, and have private conversations—out of earshot of adults—is becoming more important.

⊚ **Tweens may be more protective about their space** if they have siblings because their room becomes a personal kingdom that sets them apart.

SEE RELATED TOPICS
I don't need a babysitter: pp.190–191
I'm turning vegan: pp.192–193

WANTING TIME ALONE DOESN'T MEAN YOUR TWEEN IS HIDING ANYTHING.

HOW YOU COULD RESPOND

In the moment

Respect their need
Wanting time alone doesn't mean your tween is hiding anything—they are just becoming independent. Giving them space helps them feel trusted. They are becoming happy in their own company. If they ask you to knock, respect it. Siblings may see a sign as a challenge so encourage them to have an open-door policy sometimes.

Monitor time spent alone
Watch out for your tween spending long periods alone in their bedroom, as this could be a sign they are ruminating or struggling with their mood. Check in regularly and find ways to involve them in family activities.

Gadget-free zone
Tweens do not have the impulse control to be left alone on gadgets. Avoid giving tweens consoles, phones, or tablets they can take to their rooms and use out of view. Tell them gadgets can be used only in common areas.

In the long term

Avoid snooping
Going into their room to spy may be a sign that parents don't feel connected enough, research has found. When adolescents find adults searching through their things without permission, they become secretive. Instead, look for regular ways to spend time with your tween so they can share their thoughts and interests with you.

Respect it as their room
As your child's safe space and a place that reflects their evolving personality, listen to their opinion on how their room should look. See it as a gallery of their changing interests. Now this room is "their" space, agree on some basic expectations for your tween about keeping it tidy.

Give them protected space
If your tween shares their bedroom with a sibling, give them a place or area where they can put their things out of bounds of brothers and sisters.

POCKET **MONEY**

Financial habits are formed in the early tween years, so teaching money management now is an essential life skill that will teach tweens how to spend responsibly as adults.

Money is an abstract issue for tweens to grasp, not least because as we move toward a cashless society they are less likely to be able to touch and count coins and notes in the traditional way. By giving tweens a weekly allowance—and showing them how to stick to it and how to save—you can help them develop impulse control, learn to delay gratification, improve their money-management skills, and make wiser decisions. Acting as a good role model, by showing them how you spend and save, is an important part of their learning too.

1
Pay them a "salary"
Research shows that children's money skills are better when they get regular pocket money. Pay a fixed "wage" on the same day each week, and tell them it's their responsibility how they spend it. If you can, pay some in cash or coins.

4
Set challenges
Give them challenges, such as figuring out the cost of a home-cooked meal compared to a restaurant. Explain that money can be saved by being careful about turning off appliances.

6
Chat about collectibles
Some tweens collect toys or stickers. If your tween is building a collection, suggest they save for one a month instead of splurging on the whole set at once.

WORKING THINGS OUT

8 key principles

2

Let them see you budget
Show them your monthly budget and how you divide it up for essentials. Let them help you calculate what you have left over. Explain the difference between "needs" and "wants." Talk about something you are saving for and explain how you do that.

3

Help them develop impulse control
With money, children can learn patience, willpower, and to delay gratification. Suggest that they check in with themselves before making a purchase. Tweens have the ability to consider the future, so you could point out: "It's your money, but if you spend it all today, you won't be able to buy anything else until your next pocket money." They will discover that saving for something they really want feels better than splurging.

5

Explain borrowing
Be clear that your tween will have to save up if they want more than their weekly allowance. If they ask for extra money, explain that you will charge them interest, in the same way as a bank would.

7

Spot advertising techniques
Watch ads with your tween, and ask how they make them feel. Encourage them to spot advertising methods such as humor, slogans, jingles, animals, and celebrities.

8

Set up a savings account
Research shows that children who are encouraged to save are far more likely to keep saving as grown-ups and it gets easier with practice. Whether with coins, or by looking on their online money app—which come with kids' payment cards—show them how to separate their cash into two lots: one for spending and one for saving for rainy-day emergencies, charity donations, or items they really want. Praise them for their self-control.

TAILORED ADVICE

8–10
YEARS OLD

Use some coins
Although we are moving toward a cashless society, pay tweens their pocket money in cash, so they understand what it means. When you use a card, explain it's the same as having the cash taken out of your account.

Play board games
Have fun with money-based board games like Monopoly and Pay Day, which teach kids about concepts such as debt, mortgages, and planning.

10–12
YEARS OLD

"Employ" them
While research shows it's not a good idea to pay kids for things they should be doing anyway, such as cleaning rooms, they could increase their "salary" by doing odd jobs, such as car washing. Young people are more careful with money they have earned.

Involve them
Talk about money so it's not taboo. Ask your tween to guess the bill when you eat out—was it worth it? Ask them to help you find the best prices when you shop online.

"HOW EXACTLY ARE BABIES MADE?"

Your tween will have a general idea about how babies are conceived, but they may ask you to clear up any details that don't make sense. Filling in the gaps can feel uncomfortable because you may worry about saying the wrong thing.

SCENARIO | While in the car with you (so there is no escape!), your tween asks you exactly how babies are made.

Even though your tween is likely to know some of the mechanics, the concept of sex probably still feels confusing and embarrassing. As we raise our children from babyhood and value their innocence, we tend to believe it's our job to protect them from sex, so it can feel odd to be going into more detail.

But the fact that many children now see porn at an early age means it's important to be a trusted source of information. Even though it will be several years before they are ready for sex, see these chats as a way to help them have more fulfilling and respectful sexual relationships in the future.

WHAT YOU MIGHT BE THINKING

You may feel uncomfortable talking about sex, knowing your tween will begin to think about how they were conceived. You may be concerned they are too young for the details.

WHAT THEY MIGHT BE THINKING

⊙ **Your child may be confused** because they have figured out that sex is a taboo subject, yet it's supposed to be pleasurable.

⊙ **As they become more conscious of their bodies**, they may struggle to imagine how a penis goes into a vagina and how a baby comes out. They may use magical thinking to try to connect the dots on the parts they don't understand.

⊙ **Your tween may struggle with the "yucky" idea** of you having sex to conceive them and be confused as to why adults have intercourse when they don't want to make a baby.

⊙ **If they have romantic feelings for peers**, they might start to worry that sex is something they will be expected to do in the years to come and be concerned about common myths they have heard from other tweens, such as "getting pregnant" from kissing or holding hands.

HOW YOU COULD RESPOND

In the moment

Get the specifics
Thank them for asking, then say something like, "Tell me what you're wondering so I know where to begin." This will help you to spot any "misunderstandings" you need to clear up and decide at what level to pitch your answer.

Go slowly
Address each question directly, rather than overloading your tween with detail. If you try to get the conversation out of the way quickly, your child won't get the chance to digest what they've learned. Gauge how much further you need to venture by asking:

"Does this make sense? Are you wondering about anything else?"

Be open
If you are too embarrassed to talk about it, you are sending a message that sex is taboo. If you're unsure about how to answer, say you'd like time to think about it but do come back to them reasonably quickly. If you get it wrong, it's fine to say you'd like a chance to explain it better. If you need help, look for resources, such as age-appropriate books, to read together and that your child can go back to in their own time.

In the long term

Educate them
See these conversations as opportunities to educate your child about sex before the porn industry does so that they can separate fact from fiction. Say that if they see porn, it's likely to be shocking and you'd like them to tell you so you can put it in context for them.

Keep the door open
Make it clear to your child that they can always come to you for reliable information and they shouldn't feel scared or embarrassed. Get both parents involved, so they hear all perspectives, and get the message across that the discussion is never off-limits.

SEE RELATED TOPICS

My friend showed me this video on their phone: pp.158–159
They asked me for a nude picture: pp.194–195

" "

MAKE IT CLEAR THEY CAN ALWAYS COME TO YOU FOR RELIABLE INFORMATION.

"BUT **DAD** SAID I COULD!"

If two parents are at odds about the basic rules in the home, it can be frustrating at best and damaging at worst. The result can be resentment and distance between you as a couple, and it can be confusing and unsettling for your tween.

SCENARIO | Your partner goes against your wishes and lets your tween play their game console on a school night. You argue in front of your child.

People tend to come to parenting with different ideas about how children should be raised, depending on what they felt did or did not work for them. One parent may find it harder than the other to say no to a tween because of insecurity, guilty feelings, or a fear of conflict. This may lead the other partner to parent in opposition and take a harder line. Over time, this means one parent can get cast in the role of the "tough" parent, while the other becomes the "softer" one. The main points of conflict between parents tend to be sugary treats, screen time, and sleep schedules.

WHAT YOU MIGHT BE THINKING

You may resent your partner being the "fun" parent, and be angry that not sticking to your rules will make parenting harder. You may be conflicted about whether to be the spoilsport or just to let it go.

WHAT THEY MIGHT BE THINKING

⊚ **Your tween is likely to have figured out** that your partner is prepared to be more lax over video games and want to make the most of this opportunity.

⊚ **They know that both they and their other parent** could get into trouble, but the instant gratification of playing a video game feels better in the moment.

⊚ **While your tween will feel guilty if you both argue** about the issue, they also know it will be a useful distraction away from their behavior.

⊚ **If you start to disagree angrily in front of your tween**, it will diminish the authority of both of you in their eyes. Unconsciously they may be playing "divide and rule," taking advantage of your differences of opinion to get what they want. If you don't form a united front, they may use it as an ongoing strategy

◆ **SEE RELATED TOPICS** ◆
Just one more game: pp.36–37
I didn't think you'd mind: pp.74–75

REMEMBER THAT PARENTING IS ALL ABOUT TEAMWORK, WHICH REQUIRES DIFFERENT STRENGTHS.

HOW YOU COULD RESPOND

In the moment

Discuss in private
Avoid undermining your partner in front of your tween. Agree that your tween should stop playing in 10 minutes or at the end of the game and not on school nights.

Reaffirm the situation
If your child wants to continue playing, and says: "Dad said I could," reply: "Sometimes Dad and I can do things a bit differently, but we now agree it's best not to play it on a school night."

Discuss later
After your tween is in bed, discuss it and keep an open mind. Ask how the evening went and find out how your child ended up being allowed to play the video game.

Find a middle way
Maybe your partner would like you to be more relaxed about this. The important thing is that what you decide is consistent and that you don't undermine each other.

In the long term

Don't "compensate" for your partner
If you tend to be a "strict" parent and you feel your partner is being too lax, don't become stricter to make up for it.

Beware of divide and rule
If, at a different time, your child says, "But Dad said I could!" answer, "He may have, but I'm the one responsible for looking after you right now."

Reframe your differences
See the differences between you and your partner as a positive thing. Remember that parenting is all about teamwork, which requires different strengths. Sit down and discuss your views on the major flashpoints—and try to understand where each of your beliefs stem from.

"I WAS ONLY **JOKING!**"

As part of your child's necessary separation from you on their journey to adulthood, they may make rude comments to their parents, not realizing how hurtful they can be. When challenged, they are likely to claim that they were "only joking."

SCENARIO | Your tween says the yellow jacket you are wearing makes you look "like a Teletubby," before adding, "I was only joking!"

At this age, your tween is likely to have a stronger circle of peers around them. As they start to find their "tribe," subconsciously they may no longer feel as dependent on you as they once did and, as a result, they may experiment with being more cheeky. Dads, who may be used to being on the receiving end of jibes as part of male friendships, may not mind too much about disrespectful remarks at their expense, while moms may feel more sensitive. Moms may also be on the receiving end of more mean comments, as boys subconsciously try to prove they are no longer as reliant on their mothers, for fear of being teased by their male friends.

WHAT YOU MIGHT BE THINKING

Your child is likely to have looked up to you and adored you, so if this marks a change in that attitude, and targets your vulnerabilities and insecurities, you may feel hurt.

WHAT THEY MIGHT BE THINKING

⊙ **Your tween may think they can get away with being rude** or cheeky by adding "Just kidding" or "No offense" after a comment.

⊙ **They are acutely self-conscious** because they have an "imaginary audience" in their minds watching their every move, even when there's no one there. They may be rude about your style choice because they are imagining their peers teasing them about it.

⊙ **Your tween is self-centered and learning to develop empathy.** They will also have grown up believing that you are all-powerful and your feelings can't be hurt.

⊙ **If your tween feels ignored, criticized, or less favored,** these feelings may be too painful to admit, so they may divert them into rudeness to get attention, or as an outlet for hurt. Boys tend to make rude comments while girls are more likely to be sarcastic.

▶ **SEE RELATED TOPICS** ▶
It's not gross, it's funny: pp.80–81,
I am telling the truth: pp.166–167

HOW YOU COULD RESPOND

In the moment

Be curious
Ask them what they mean. You could help your child think how this comment has made you feel by responding with "Ouch" and by using "I feel" statements.

Challenge them
Question your tween's get-out clause. Tell them that a mean comment is never canceled out by adding, "Only joking" or "No offense" afterward.

Don't take it personally
Finding their parents embarrassing is part of your child's necessary separation from you on their journey to becoming an adult. Be reassured it is a phase that will pass when they are more sure of their own identity.

Be consistent
Boys are more likely to make cruel comments for the entertainment of their male peer group. It is important for all parents to call out any mean—and especially misogynistic—comments on the spot, so your tween understands they are not acceptable.

In the long term

Teach empathy
One of the best ways to help children learn the impact of their unkind words is to train them in empathy skills. Chat about how characters in movies and books might feel, as well as real-life people in the news. Be expressive, too, about how you feel in different situations.

Talk about context
Research shows that crude and mean humor is one of the ways boys bond in friendship groups, where humor, funny put-downs, and the ability to take a joke, is highly prized. Try to understand how humor is used in their friendship group, but question how they think the kind of edgy one-liners they exchange might be heard by others.

Reconnect
If these digs are repeated and personal, try to connect with your child to see what lies beneath. This behavior could be your child's way of saying they feel unhappy, rejected, or less favored in the family. Spend some fun one-on-one time together so you can bond and reset your relationship.

> ## TRAIN THEM IN EMPATHY SKILLS—CHAT ABOUT HOW CHARACTERS IN MOVIES AND BOOKS MIGHT FEEL, AS WELL AS REAL-LIFE PEOPLE IN THE NEWS.

"THEY SAY I'M A **SHOW-OFF**"

As tweens start to compare each other and social hierarchies form, some will try to impress others to win friends and for social status. But if they keep claiming to be the best, boasting can have the opposite effect.

SCENARIO | Your tween complains that others don't want to play with them at break time because they are a show-off about their soccer skills.

Your tween is now becoming more aware of how they are developing at different rates from others—and that certain skills will win admiration and respect from their peers. Social hierarchies are being formed in which a talent, like being good at sport, or some other advantage like being good-looking, may give them social power. However, this status is conferred when it is observed by other kids, not because your child tells their peers what to think. If your tween tries to impress their peers by boasting or exaggerating their skills, it will backfire.

WHAT YOU MIGHT BE THINKING

While you want your tween to be proud of what they have accomplished, you may worry that what they say is coming across as bragging, which is annoying for others.

WHAT THEY MIGHT BE THINKING

⦿ **Your tween may wrongly believe** that if other children are impressed by them, they will want to be their friend. "Magical" or "wishful" thinking may lead them to believe that if they tell others that they excel, it means they do.

⦿ **If your child has heard their parents,** or perhaps older siblings, showing off too, they may think that boasting is a normal form of social currency.

⦿ **If you have showered your tween with praise** in the hope of building their self-esteem, they may believe they are better at a particular activity than they are.

⦿ **Your tween may not realize** that coming across as superior is not an appealing trait and is likely to make them unpopular, rather than popular, with classmates.

HOW YOU COULD RESPOND

In the moment

Talk about connection
Explain to your tween that friendship is about enjoying other people's company, not proving to them how talented you are. To help them connect with other children, encourage them to find out what they have in common with others, rather than focusing on what makes them "better."

Make them aware
Tweens are still learning to imagine what others are feeling. If your child has reason to be proud, validate this but suggest they ask themself if "showing off" their accomplishments will make others feel inferior and therefore might not want to play with them.

In the long term

Suggest actions speak louder
If your tween really does excel at soccer, for example, others are likely to want to play with them because it will be fun. However, their peers are likely to be irritated and make fun of them if there is a big gap between how good your child says they are at soccer, and the reality. Say to your tween that it may be better to "show, not tell."

Talk about skills
Explain that everyone has a special skill, and that all are valuable. While one person may be good at sports, for example, another classmate's strength may be math or drawing. Everyone is different.

Be realistic
Research has found that parents who often tell their children they are more "special" than others can give them an inflated self-image. Instead of showering your tween with exaggerated praise, notice and acknowledge what they do well.

SEE RELATED TOPICS
I got the best grade: pp.88–89
I'm a loser: pp.92–93

" "

TELL YOUR TWEEN IT'S BETTER TO "SHOW, NOT TELL."

"I'VE GOT **NOTHING TO DO**"

If your tween is usually kept busy with a lot of extracurricular activities and is used to playing on screens a lot, they may find themself feeling bored and at a loss when they have free time on their hands. Their go-to activity may always be screen time.

SCENARIO | Your tween has downtime at home and can't think of anything to do because they have exceeded their daily screen-time limit.

It can be tempting to give children a screen to play on to keep them occupied when they need a break. Over time, as they get older, the flashing lights, changing colors, and constantly changing stimuli of screen entertainment becomes an easy ready-made way to occupy themself, giving their brain's reward system an instant dopamine hit. Nonscreen activities, such as reading, playing real-world games, and doing arts and crafts, take more time and effort and therefore may be less appealing in the immediate present. But it is worth encouraging these nonscreen activities.

WHAT YOU MIGHT BE THINKING

You might be annoyed that with plenty of books and games on hand, your tween is only interested in screens. You may think you aren't doing enough to keep your child busy and feel pressured to fix the problem.

◆ **SEE RELATED TOPICS** ◆
Are we there yet?: pp.20–21
Why can't I go on TikTok?: pp.124–125

WHAT THEY MIGHT BE THINKING

⊙ **If your tween is used to using a screen** as a default whenever they have free time, they may find it hard to focus on any activity that doesn't offer the same instant gratification and sense of control. They may be interpreting feelings of discomfort as "boredom."

⊙ **Tween brains are particularly wired for novelty.** It means that for a child brought up digesting fast-moving images, pages of text in a book may feel dull because they don't give them an immediate visual reward.

⊙ **Saying that they are bored** may be a way of your tween saying they feel ignored or disconnected from you and that they would like your attention.

⊙ **If your child attends a lot of after-school activities**, they may not be in the habit of entertaining themself for periods of time at home without screens.

HOW YOU COULD RESPOND

In the moment

Acknowledge their feelings
Say you know that being bored feels uncomfortable, but it will pass. Encourage them to give their brain time to come up with what they would like to do next.

Dig a little deeper
Listen to what lies beneath your child's statement. Are they really at a loose end, or do they want your attention? Are they too tired to find their own entertainment? Do they need encouragement to come up with ideas?

Become available
If you think they feel lonely, ask if they'd like to help you with a task, or to do something together.

Avoid offering solutions
Rather than solve the problem, ask questions to help them notice where their interests lead them.

Avoid offering a screen
Offering them a screen will prevent them from using their imagination and finding things to do. And saying no next time will be harder.

In the long term

Have an ideas jar
At the start of school vacation, list activities your child would like to do on pieces of paper and put them in a jar. They can pick one when they are bored. Once they start reading or crafting, discuss the satisfaction of finishing a chapter or a project stage.

Take gadget breaks
Head to your library or bookstore and ask your child to choose a book with no direction from you. Then visit a café for a hot chocolate and read. Or let them choose a project in the craft store.

Read with them
Once children can read fluently, it's easy to leave them to it. But when parents read with tweens, they understand more vocabulary and are more likely to love books and return to them when alone.

Value downtime
Let go of guilt about always entertaining your child. Rather than see it as "wasted" time, see free time as a chance to let your child's mind wander without pressure to achieve anything. Boredom is a sign they have time to try something new.

> RATHER THAN SEEING IT AS "WASTED" TIME, BOREDOM IS A SIGN THEY HAVE TIME TO TRY SOMETHING NEW.

"ALL MY FRIENDS HAVE A PHONE"

To a tween, getting their first phone feels like a rite of passage and a passport to a new world of fun and freedom. As a parent, you are likely to have some reservations.

SCENARIO | Your tween pleads for a smartphone for their birthday because "all their friends have one."

For a tween, a phone is like all the toys wrapped into one. They can play exciting games, take photos, and message friends. If many peers have one, it will be the ultimate status symbol in their group. Your tween won't see a phone as the door to an adult world into which they are too young to venture alone. If you're not able to talk to your child about the dangers of seeing porn or being approached by strangers online, then your child is not ready for a phone. If you want to give your child a phone, be prepared to put clear guidelines in place and to monitor their use until they are ready to go it alone.

WHAT YOU MIGHT BE THINKING

You may feel conflicted: you don't want them to have a phone yet but are worried they will miss out socially if all their friends have one.

◀ **SEE RELATED TOPICS** ▶

They posted a mean message: pp.114–115
Why can't I go on TikTok?: pp.124–125

WHAT THEY MIGHT BE THINKING

◉ **Your child is so fixated on the prize of getting a phone** that they will beg you as if their life depends on it. They know their safety is your priority so will persuade you by saying that you will be able to get hold of them at any time.

◉ **They can see only the upsides** and, unlike you, they won't worry about losing real-world interaction and being exposed to possible adult content and danger.

◉ **They are more invested in relationships with peers** and want to be able to message their friends out of school.

◉ **Your tween will believe that having a phone** will make them look more grown-up and therefore more powerful.

HELP THEM BUILD A POSITIVE SOCIAL MEDIA FEED BASED ON THEIR INTERESTS.

HOW YOU COULD RESPOND

In the moment

Hear them out
Listen to your tween's request so they know that you are taking them seriously.

Make them aware
Tweens often assume phones are a human right rather than something to prove they are ready for. Tell them how much a phone costs and that it is a privilege to have one.

Educate them
Explain that phones are not toys, and you will monitor what they use it for and how much time they spend on it. Explain that you will be there alongside them, as with a student driver, until they can take control by themself.

Empathize
If the time is not right, give them in fantasy what you can't give them in reality. Try saying: "I know a phone would make you feel grown-up, but I want you to grow up experiencing life in the real world first."

In the long term

Find a middle way
If they are not ready for their own phone, allow them to use an old family phone or tablet that you all access.

Focus on the good
When you do allow them to have a phone, help them build a positive social media feed based on their interests and find child-friendly news sites. Show them how to block, unfollow, and report accounts that make them feel uncomfortable.

Put up guardrails
Tweens welcome protection against things they don't want to see, so at this stage they won't mind parent controls. Allow them to post pictures only to closed groups of friends and family, not on public forums, which will satisfy most kids this age. Limit time on phones to an hour a day after homework is done, which is the safest amount. Agree to a contract that includes no phones at meals or alone in bedrooms. Phones must also be handed to you to charge overnight.

CLIMATE CHANGE

Your tween will be starting to get an understanding of the world beyond their community. At the same time, they will be hearing about climate change and wondering what it means for their future.

The dawning realization that the planet is overheating, and that humans caused this, may shake your child's belief that the world is a safe place. They will take their cues from you, so do your best to calm your own worries first and model a hopeful and constructive approach to this issue. Research shows that the best antidote to worrying is doing something about the issue, and young people who are concerned, yet optimistic, do the most to look after the planet. Listening to your child's concerns and supporting them in taking some action, however small, will help them feel heard and empowered.

1
Allay feelings of blame
When issues aren't explained, tweens use magical thinking to fill gaps. Putting themselves at the center of the story, they may believe that going on a plane means they are to blame for climate change.

4
Offer hope
Remind your tween that climate change is a long process, and scientists and politicians are speeding up efforts to find solutions. Our understanding of solutions are constantly evolving.

6
Help them develop skills
Show them how to be change-makers in simple ways: making a bird feeder, growing bee-friendly plants in a window box, picking up litter, or rewilding a green space.

WORKING THINGS OUT

8 key principles

2
Listen to their concerns
Acknowledge their fears and feelings, and listen to what they have to say. You could say: "Yes, it's scary to think about the planet changing. But there are many steps we're all taking to make things better, such as recycling and driving less."

3
Show them how people are helping
Give them hope by talking about how humankind has evolved to be clever and resourceful and has survived other challenges, like quickly developing vaccines to control COVID-19. Show them how lots of clever people are already coming up with great ideas.

5
Connect them with community activities
Tweens may feel powerless to make a difference. Show what other young people, like Greta Thunberg, who started her climate strike action movement while still at school, have achieved—especially when they band together to make their voices heard. Ask your tween if they'd like to join up with other youth activists in your community or online.

7
Process your own worries
Tweens look to caregivers to see how much they should be worried. Process your own fears with other parents and climate change activists so you can be a solid support. Band together so tweens can see that you belong to a community of caring adults.

8
Show them you care
Your tween may feel angry that their generation has inherited the task of "fixing this" and feel like adults are to blame. Show them what you are doing to take care of the planet, too, whether it's fitting solar panels or reducing meat and dairy intake.

TAILORED ADVICE

8–10 YEARS OLD

Encourage good habits
Research shows that routines are formed by the age of nine, so turning off lights and recycling will stick with kids if they are shown these habits early in life.

Get outdoors
The more time your child spends in nature, the better they will understand how to protect it. Find simple outdoor activities, such as going on an insect safari, taking paper and crayons on a walk to do a tree bark rubbing, or noticing the changing seasons.

10–12 YEARS OLD

Reassure them
Validate your child's feelings in these uncertain times, and acknowledge that they are a natural part of growing up and wanting to take care of the planet and its animals. Talk to them about how their concerns will inspire them, and others, to act.

Notice good news
The news agenda is skewed toward dramatic incidents of bad news. Talk about the inventions and advances people are making worldwide.

"I AM DOING MY HOMEWORK"

Homework steps up a gear as tweens progress through school. But after a long day of lessons, they can find it difficult to get down to homework tasks and complete them.

SCENARIO | Your child is struggling to finish the math questions they have been assigned for homework.

Getting tweens to complete homework can become a regular flashpoint. Your tween is still developing the executive functions in their brain's prefrontal cortex that help them delay gratification and do things they don't want to do. They are only just developing the ability to plan long term, so homework may feel pointless, rather than a discipline that forms good habits for the future.

WHAT YOU MIGHT BE THINKING

After several reminders, you might get frustrated by your child delaying homework. You're desperate for them to finish so that you can all relax.

SEE RELATED TOPICS
I just can't sit still: pp.68–69
I'm scared I won't get
a good grade: pp.138–139

WHAT THEY MIGHT BE THINKING

◉ **If they find math hard, they may avoid it.** Anything can become a distraction. If they are on a computer, they may be tempted by online games if you can't see their screen.

◉ **Without a teacher, your tween may not know where to start.** Their lesson on this topic might feel like it was a long time ago. They might be worried that they won't be able to apply what they were taught.

◉ **They may feel pressure to get the answers right.** The fright-flight-freeze part of their brain might have been triggered, making it harder for them to think logically. It may feel easier not to try at all than to try and fail.

◉ **Your tween may hope you will do it for them** if they drag it out long enough. Or if it worked before, they might hope you will give them treats for finishing their homework.

> **"** **"**
> ## ONCE HOMEWORK BECOMES A HABIT, YOU WILL MEET LESS RESISTANCE.

HOW YOU COULD RESPOND

In the moment

Suggest dipping a toe in
When a task is daunting, the most difficult part is starting. Suggest doing just five minutes at first. The likelihood is that they will keep going.

Teach self-management
Use a timer. This will help tweens visualize how long their homework session should last, reinforcing the idea that it shouldn't swallow up hours of time. Point out that they can do fun activities as soon as it's finished.

Clarify the issue
Help your child vocalize the reasons they are struggling. Suggest: "Do you need reminding how to do multiplication?" Once you have listened and understood, they are more likely to get on with it.

Hold the line
As tempting as it is to help your child finish their homework, resist. It sends a message that they are not capable and that you will always rescue them from uncomfortable challenges.

In the long term

Remind them that they can do hard things
Talk about another skill they found hard at first but mastered with perseverance, whether it's reading chapter books or learning to skateboard.

Find a routine
The later it gets, the harder it will be to start homework. At a neutral time, ask your child how long they need to rest after school and when would be a good time to start homework. Once it becomes a habit, at the same time each day, you will meet less resistance.

Set up a regular spot
Your tween could do their homework somewhere close to you—perhaps at the kitchen table—and free of distractions, such as toys and electronics.

See the bigger picture
Teachers often say how long homework tasks should take. If your child struggles to complete it within the time, consider getting them assessed for learning challenges. It's best to identify any issues early.

"I JUST CAN'T SIT STILL"

As children get older, their ability to concentrate and sit still tends to increase. But if your parent–teacher meetings are turning into a string of complaints that your child is lacking focus, you will need to find out why.

SCENARIO | You ask your tween why the teacher says they don't concentrate in class—they tell you they find it hard to sit still.

By the age of eight, a child's average attention span is 16–24 minutes. By age 10, it's about 20–30 minutes. Of course, all youngsters will have challenges paying attention to teachers and parents sometimes—and there may be many reasons why a child struggles to focus on a task, from tiredness to anxiety to boredom or lack of interest. But if your child's ability to concentrate lags behind their classmates for more than a few months, and their schoolwork and self-esteem start to suffer, it may help to find out why. Otherwise, tweens can start to drop behind—or give up.

WHAT YOU MIGHT BE THINKING

You might wonder if they will grow out of this phase and worry about what will happen to their progress at school if they don't.

" "
CONSIDER WHETHER DIET IS CREATING BLOOD-SUGAR HIGHS AND LOWS AND WHETHER THEY ARE EXERCISING ENOUGH.

◀ **SEE RELATED TOPICS** ▶
I am doing my homework: pp.66–67
I don't want to go to school: pp.108–109

WHAT THEY MIGHT BE THINKING

⊙ **Sitting still and listening in class may be understimulating.** Fidgeting could be their way of drawing focus back to the task.

⊙ **Your child may know that others find fidgeting annoying,** but they still can't stop because they are so easily distracted—perhaps by what's going on outside, any worries, or what other children are doing.

⊙ **They might compare themself to other children.** As they drop behind in areas of learning, they may avoid tasks that feel difficult or uncomfortable and brand themself stupid.

HOW YOU COULD RESPOND

In the moment

Boost their self-esteem
Tell them their ability to maintain concentration is separate from their intelligence. Talk about their strengths and accomplishments and times when they find it easier to concentrate, so they don't feel judged by their performance in class. Every child wants to try, but they may decide it's not worth trying if they keep failing.

Dig deeper
Rule out any psychological or physical reasons; ask if they are being bullied or if anything is making them anxious. Ask if they have aches or pains that are bothering them. Consider whether diet is creating blood-sugar highs and lows and whether they are exercising enough to

disperse any built-up stress hormones. Make sure they are getting enough sleep—even 30 minutes less sleep can make it harder to manage restlessness.

Look at overall behavior
Is your child fidgety at home? Do they have difficulty getting down to and sticking to homework but seem more focused on pastimes they are really interested in?

Be curious
Explain that everyone's brain works differently. Ask what classes are like for them, and if repetitive thoughts or any sensory stimulus, such as smells or sounds, distract them. Ask when they find it easiest and hardest to concentrate.

In the long term

Suggest alternatives
Find ways they could fidget less obviously, such as tapping their fingers against their own hands, squeezing their toes inside their shoes, or doodling.

Get an assessment
Once you have ruled out health or emotional issues, get your child professionally tested for any learning challenges. One possibility may be ADHD—Attention Deficit Hyperactivity

Disorder—that makes it more difficult to maintain and control attention due to lower levels of some brain neurotransmitters.

Be vigilant with screens
When tweens are learning to focus, screens make it harder for them to concentrate for longer periods. Studies have found links between early screen use and shorter attention spans. Screen time has been found to make ADHD symptoms worse.

"I DIDN'T HIT THEM"

While sibling conflict is a normal part of family life, it can escalate in the tween years as children become more physically powerful and start to compare and compete with one another. You may increasingly find yourself in the role of referee.

SCENARIO | Your tween denies hitting their younger sibling during a disagreement about who has the TV remote.

Siblings spend more time together than with any other children. This constant proximity, a lack of impulse control, and competing for your attention, can often turn your family home into a battle zone.

While friendships with peers come and go, your child knows their siblings aren't going anywhere—and their familiarity with each other means they know how to trigger one another easily. However grating sibling conflict can be, see it as an opportunity to teach your children about negotiation and compromise.

WHAT YOU MIGHT BE THINKING

You may feel torn between your children because you want to be fair, but you will find it hard to referee fights that started out of your sight.

WHAT THEY MIGHT BE THINKING

◉ **Your tween is discovering their strength,** and if they find their younger siblings more irritating, they may use their force to get their way. They may also take out their general frustrations on siblings.

◉ **Your tween will feel like the fight is for your love** and approval once you intervene. They are likely to say anything to get themself out of trouble.

◉ **If your tween admits to hitting their younger sibling,** they will claim repeatedly that they were provoked, believing this will justify their behavior.

◉ **If their sibling is hurt, they may cry** to deal with feelings of guilt and being overwhelmed, and try to gain sympathy.

◆ **SEE RELATED TOPICS** ◆
We were just pretending: pp.76–77
I didn't mean to punch the wall: pp.176–177

HOW YOU COULD RESPOND

In the moment

Resist being the referee
Unless you witnessed the argument from the start, it's impossible to know what happened. If you take sides, you will also increase resentment and one child will feel like the winner and the other, the loser. Instead, see this as an opportunity to help them both learn problem-solving and negotiation skills.

Speak to both children
Bear in mind that you missed what led to the incident. Rather than rush to place blame, acknowledge both children by saying: "I see two kids having a difficult time."

Offer empathy
If you believe one child has been hurt, tell them: "That must have been horrible to be hit. I am here now." To the other, you could say, "Do you see your sibling crying? I know you wouldn't want to hurt someone. What's happening for you?" When they are calm, ask them to name how they feel and encourage them to suggest other ways they could have resolved the issue.

Emphasize family values
While sibling conflict is normal, make it clear that using force and mean words is never acceptable. Make it a family value that everyone has a right to feel safe.

In the long term

View it differently
If there is no deliberate and ongoing violence, and most of the time the siblings are evenly matched, remember that sibling conflict is normal. Be reassured that if things are harmonious most of the time they are together, you're on the right track.

Teach anger management
If a tween often gets annoyed and lashes out at younger siblings, help them find ways to manage their feelings, like kicking a ball in the back of a net, finding a grown-up to talk to, or distracting themself by listening to music or doing a hobby.

"THEY DIDN'T SAVE ME A SEAT AT LUNCHTIME"

Parents tend to worry about their child being bullied.
However, more common are day-to-day power plays inside
friendship groups, known as relational aggression,
where children may feel excluded.

SCENARIO | Your tween tells you their friends were whispering at break time, then they didn't save them a seat at lunchtime.

Even within groups of friends, there are power struggles. Each member will unconsciously fall into a hierarchy, often with someone at the top. Conflict can flare if members try to teach each other a lesson for breaking the unwritten rules of the group, or flex their social status to marginalize others. If a decision is made by two or more members that someone is "annoying," the target can be deliberately left out.

WHAT YOU MIGHT BE THINKING

You may worry about the impact on your child and think about contacting the parents of the other kids to sort it out. It may trigger similar childhood memories for you.

SEE RELATED TOPICS
I don't want to go to school: pp.108–109
My teacher hates me!: pp.146–147

WHAT THEY MIGHT BE THINKING

⊙ **Your tween is forming their identity** outside the family, so the pain of peer rejection is great. They may be tearful, find it hard to concentrate, and may not want to go to school.

⊙ **They will be confused about how to respond.** Passive-aggressive tactics like no longer saving seats are hard to pin down, because the friends may claim it is not deliberate and that your child is being "oversensitive."

⊙ **They may still want to be friends with the same children,** even if the exclusion is deliberate, because they would rather put up with being treated badly than be cast out of the group altogether.

⊙ **Your tween may know the factors that led up to this** moment, if there has been tension, but may only tell you one side of the story. They want your sympathy and don't want to cast themself in a bad light.

HOW YOU COULD RESPOND

In the moment

Make time to listen
Resist the temptation to give advice or criticize your child's friends. Spend time with your tween so they feel loved and safe with you.

Put it in perspective
While empathizing with your child's situation, bear in mind the research that shows that politics and power plays happen inside every friendship group and social conflict is normal.

Help divert them
If they genuinely don't know the reason they are being excluded, your tween is likely to be replaying all the moments that led up to this. Once you've talked these through, offer to help pivot your child to a favorite activity so they don't keep ruminating on the reasons.

In the long term

Make them self-aware
It's important for your child to identify healthy relationships now and in the future. When they're not upset, ask them how they feel in their friendship group. Explain that all friendships have ups and downs, but if they often feel left out, it's time to find new friends.

Look for patterns
Do they often claim they have no one to play with? Do they struggle with social skills, noticing social cues, and behave in ways others find annoying or clingy? With support, they can improve these skills and relationships.

Help them find a new group
If they decide to move on, suggest they avoid any showdowns with old friends, and take time to get to know others. Remind them that friendship is a transaction: if they show friendly interest, others usually return it. Suggest that they join a new school club to widen their circle.

"I DIDN'T THINK YOU'D MIND"

The prefrontal cortex of your tween's brain, which helps them restrain from impulsive actions, is still getting wired up. So in the moment, if they want something badly and it will impress their peers, they may find it hard to control themself.

SCENARIO | You've discovered your child has bought virtual currency, without your permission, to get ahead of their friends in a video game.

Video games may be a key part of your tween's social life, and skill and success can win them social capital. To monetize games, players are offered the chance to make purchases to give their characters superpowers to progress faster. Some of these take the form of loot boxes, or virtual treasure chests, which players pay for with real-world money, without knowing what's inside. In their excitement in the moment and determination to get ahead, tweens may feel driven to make such purchases. Unless you apply controls with care, your child can click on these, charging the payment to your credit card.

WHAT YOU MIGHT BE THINKING

When you see the charge come up on your bank statement, you may be shocked, furious, and feel "robbed" by your own child.

WHAT THEY MIGHT BE THINKING

◉ **Your tween is still learning how money works** and that it can be transferred virtually. As the money is offered in the game's own currency, they may not fully understand that you are the one paying for the purchase with real money.

◉ **Your child may think you have unlimited amounts of money** to spend and that you won't notice. Or they may have used wishful thinking to persuade themself that they don't have to pay.

◉ **Tweens don't know whether the reward will be big or small.** This gives them the "slot machine effect"—a bigger rush of dopamine if the win they are paying for turns out to be greater than expected.

◉ **Your child is likely to feel shocked and ashamed** when they realize what they have done because they find it painful to disappoint you.

❝ ❞

MAKE MONEY REAL FOR THEM BY SHOWING HOW YOU BUDGET EACH MONTH.

HOW YOU COULD RESPOND

In the moment

Calm yourself
Manage your emotions by taking deep breaths and letting the first wave of anger and dismay pass over you. By modeling emotional regulation, you are setting a good example, and your child is more likely to come to you with any digital problems in the future.

Check parental controls
In their drive to win the game, the temptation could always prove too much. Until your tween has learned to better control their impulses, install double authentication controls to make sure they cannot spend money without your permission.

Apply consequences
While this is likely to have been a mistake or a judgment failure, find a way for your tween to make amends by paying back the money they spent, either from their money box or their pocket money. This will help them to understand how long it takes to earn money.

In the long term

Explain credit cards
Help your tween understand that once they purchase virtual gaming rewards online, you can't get the money back. Make money real for them by showing how you budget for the month and what you have to allocate for essentials, such as food and household bills.

Play the game
By playing the game with your tween, you will start to understand what is tempting them to spend, how the game lures them in, and whether you have set up strong enough parental controls.

Educate them
Younger children tend not to think of themselves as customers who can earn money for adults. For this reason, research shows that preteens are particularly vulnerable to sales and advertising. Explain how video game companies set up features, with all sorts of tricks to encourage players to spend money.

◄ SEE RELATED TOPICS ►
Just one more game: pp.36–37
Why can't I go on TikTok?: pp.124–125

"WE WERE JUST PRETENDING"

According to research, play-fighting, involving wrestling each other and rolling around, is an enjoyable activity for many tweens. While it can be noisy and sometimes worrying to watch, when done safely, rough-and-tumble play brings many benefits.

SCENARIO | On a playdate, your tween alarms you by playing a game in which they and their friend pretend to shoot each other.

Many young mammals play-fight to develop strength and learn how to assert and defend themselves. But while a love of rough-and-tumble play has evolved as a natural part of human childhood, some adults worry whether it's safe or appropriate in today's society.

Be reassured that between friends, play-fighting rarely turns into real fighting. As long as the players are fairly matched and enjoying it, see it as an opportunity for kids to practice self-restraint and give-and-take skills. Research consistently shows that boys are far more drawn to rough-and-tumble play than girls.

WHAT YOU MIGHT BE THINKING

You may worry that someone is going to get hurt. You may wonder where they got the idea from and think that if you don't intervene, your tween will think it's okay to be aggressive.

WHAT THEY MIGHT BE THINKING

◉ **Rough-and-tumble play feels like the opportunity for boys**, in particular, to show off their developing strength, speed, and coordination, and to test boundaries.

◉ **Children this age tend to view using a loud, bellowing voice** as a way to scare their "enemies," whereas you might hear shouts of "got you" and "you're dead" as annoying and disruptive.

◉ **Your tween may be bewildered by any objections** because they know their game is make-believe. If you say you disapprove of it, they might feel you disapprove of them too.

◉ **Research shows that older tweens**, who now know their physical strength, might start to use play-fighting as a way to assert physical dominance over weaker children and strengthen their place in the social hierarchy.

HOW YOU COULD RESPOND

In the moment

Consider the benefits
Studies have found no link between play-fighting and real-life aggression but have found that play-fighting can help children regulate their emotions and is a safe outlet for anger and a way to learn to read body language.

Suggest some ground rules
Ask your tween and their playmate to agree to a "stop" word, which will halt play if the game becomes too much, or one player needs a break: "When you say 'stop,' I have to stop. When I say 'stop,' you have to stop."

Be vigilant
It may be noisy and sound threatening, but play-fighting is safe if everyone involved is laughing, they are taking turns being the winners and losers, and they want to keep playing after the "battle." Watch out for one child always being on the receiving end, being pinned down, showing signs of distress, or who is socially further down the pecking order.

In the long term

Give them free rein
Provide safe opportunities for your tween to play physical games. If they can't go outside, give them alternative safe places to play indoors. Make it a rule that they have to put everything back afterward.

Take it outside
Children will have more freedom and you will worry less if they can play outside. In the natural world, they are also more likely to team up together to fight an imaginary common enemy than to fight each other.

For moms and dads
Research shows that tweens love rough-and-tumble play with dads especially, who tend to have had more practice. But playing physical games and chasing games can be fun and bonding for moms too.

SEE RELATED TOPICS
I was only joking: pp.56–57
I didn't hit them: pp.70–71

PLAY-FIGHTING CAN HELP CHILDREN REGULATE THEIR EMOTIONS.

"ARE YOU GOING TO **DIE** TOO?"

Your tween may be starting to understand that death is forever.
Though it may be a painful topic, the loss of a grandparent
or close relative can help your child develop a deeper
understanding of life and how precious it is.

SCENARIO | You have told your child their grandma has died and they
begin to question whether you are going to die too.

By the age of seven or eight, you may notice your child is beginning to think more logically. They will have seen animals or insects die and be aware that death is irreversible. However, the concept of death, and the fact that it happens to everyone, will still seem unfathomable and overwhelming.

As your tween starts to think more hypothetically, they may have lots of questions. Uppermost in their minds will be whether other adults, like parents, could also die, leaving no one to care for them. Giving clear, honest information will help put their minds at rest.

WHAT YOU MIGHT BE THINKING

If you believe your child is too young to be told about the reality of death, you may be tempted to use euphemisms, such as "Grandma's gone to sleep" or "She's gone to a better place."

WHAT THEY MIGHT BE THINKING

⊚ **Now that tweens have better memories** than when they were younger, they will have clearer recollections of the time they spent with their grandma and miss her when they realize they won't see her again.

⊚ **Having believed you were invulnerable,** your child now realizes that you won't live forever either. They may become more anxious about your health and safety.

⊚ **If they lost a loved one** when they were younger, your tween may go through a phase of "regrieving" now that they understand the finality of death.

⊚ **While your child gets used to the idea that grandma is dead,** they will see-saw emotionally, switching from being sad when they remember her and happy when they go back to living in the moment. These "islands of grief" don't mean they don't care.

SEE RELATED TOPICS
I'll be homesick: pp.22–23
I want a hug: pp.44–45

> ## GIVING CLEAR, HONEST INFORMATION WILL PUT THEIR MINDS AT REST.

HOW YOU COULD RESPOND

In the moment

Be open
While it's tempting to use euphemisms, tell the truth sensitively. According to research, when adults were asked to recall the worst lie they were told in childhood, it was not being told the truth about the death of a loved one.

Address concerns
If your tween asks if you will die, make it clear that the death of a loved one does not happen often. Explain we all die eventually and you don't expect it to happen for a long time, by which time they will be a grown-up, which will feel for them like a long time in the future.

Reassure them
Because tweens tend to put themselves at the center of every story, they might imagine that "Grandma died because I didn't do what I was told." Check that they don't have any misunderstandings. Give them permission to be happy again.

In the long term

Offer a choice about the funeral
Attending may answer questions for them and help them see that the reality of death is not as scary as they thought. They may also be comforted by the ritual and hearing others talk about their grandma in loving terms.

Be prepared for questions
Tweens may have questions about where grandma is. If you don't have a belief system that guides you, it's fine to say you don't know or to talk about how dead bodies return to the natural world.

Keep talking
If your child is showing regressive behavior, like wanting comfort items, encourage them to put their grief into words. Give your child tangible ways of mourning grandma. Look through old pictures and talk about happy memories or put together a memorial box. They could plant a tree or sponsor a wild animal in her name.

"IT'S NOT GROSS; IT'S FUNNY!"

As your tween learns what is and isn't acceptable, they may experiment with more adult humor to test boundaries. Crude or bawdy jokes may also showcase their newfound knowledge about sex and distance them from subjects that make them feel uncomfortable.

SCENARIO | After dinner, your child and their friends stay at the table, telling each other offensive toilet and dead baby jokes.

A sense of humor can make your child happier, more optimistic, more socially powerful among their peers, and more resilient. However, having learned many rules of how to behave, your tween is now also learning that it's funny to break them—and humor is one way to test the limits of what's acceptable. Tweens, especially boys, may veer into more off-color jokes to test social norms, feel more grown up, and show they are old enough to defy expectations of "nice" behavior.

WHAT YOU MIGHT BE THINKING

You may feel unsure whether to ignore your tween's jokes or to correct them. You may wonder where they got such crude humor, whether others will be offended, and how it reflects on you.

WHAT THEY MIGHT BE THINKING

◉ **They may feel good when people laugh at their jokes** and notice that it wins them popularity and respect.

◉ **Off-color jokes help tweens identify peers** who are at a similar developmental level, and they can be a way of bonding with others. Humor can also diffuse tension and offload worries about masculinity and gender.

◉ **Even if they know a joke is edgy or offensive**, the social payoff of making others laugh will make them take the risk anyway—and they will have figured out they can get themself off the hook by saying "Only joking!"

◉ **Boys may be trying on laddishness for size** when they veer into sexist jokes, to assert their masculinity and feel more grown-up. As they push boundaries, they will go too far.

HOW YOU COULD RESPOND

In the moment

Pull a face
Facial expressions that signal disgust and disapproval help children understand when they have crossed a line.

Stay measured
Rather than getting angry, be curious about what they find funny. Remember, what children find hilarious may be different from what makes adults laugh. Even if you find some of their humor offensive, listen. Humor is communication. What they find funny can tell you a lot about what's on their minds.

Emphasize good manners
Some tweens also enjoy slapstick and physical humor, like eating with their mouths open or deliberately passing wind. Hold the line on what is considered socially acceptable and explain that others will think less of them, or even avoid them, if they don't abide by basic manners.

In the long term

Talk about context
Explain that though their friends may think it's funny, others may have personal experience of the controversial subjects they are joking about and may feel hurt and offended. Tell them while you love hearing your child laugh and joke, it shouldn't be at the expense of others.

Help them develop empathy
If jokes are cruel, crude, or against groups of people, ask your tween why they think it's funny, and to think about the impact of their words. If you stay silent, they may assume you endorse the jokes.

Keep up the humor
Laughter activates reward pathways in the brain, reduces stress, and boosts the immune system, as well as being a useful way to lift a tween out of a grump. So keep humor at the heart of family life, based on in-jokes and funny memories.

SEE RELATED TOPICS
They say I'm a show-off: pp.58–59
She's a slut: pp.156–157

❝ ❞

KEEP HUMOR AT THE HEART OF FAMILY LIFE, BASED ON IN-JOKES AND FUNNY MEMORIES.

"CAN I GO ON A **SLEEPOVER?**"

For some kids, sleepovers are some of the most cherished and highly anticipated moments of the tween years. Others need a more gradual introduction to this first step toward independence. Either way, sleepovers can throw up challenges for parents.

SCENARIO | Your tween asks if they can go on their first sleepover with a close friend, even though you are not sure if they are ready for it.

Successful sleepovers can be a great way for tweens to bond with friends and learn about how other families live, how to adapt, and get practice at being independent in a controlled environment. They will also learn new skills, such as planning what they need to take, getting ready for bed without you, and communicating their needs. But, like many parents, you may worry about your child going on a sleepover, being concerned that they are not old enough to deal with unfamiliar household rules and later bedtimes, and that they don't yet have the agency to speak up for themself if they feel uncomfortable or unsettled.

WHAT YOU MIGHT BE THINKING

You may worry about disruption to your child's sleep routine, about safeguarding issues if you don't know the family, and about the activities they may do there.

WHAT THEY MIGHT BE THINKING

◉ **Sleepovers will make tweens feel grown-up** and can put the seal on a close friendship or confirm best friend status.

◉ **Your tween and their friends are likely to be anticipating** spending time in their bedroom and chatting and sharing secrets out of the hearing of grown-ups.

◉ **They will be eagerly planning the activities** they want to do together, such as midnight feasts, days in advance.

◉ **Despite the social pull, your tween may still worry** about sleeping in an unfamiliar place and whether they will feel homesick when they are there.

" "

LAY DOWN A SET OF REASONABLE RULES SO YOUR CHILD UNDERSTANDS WHAT IS EXPECTED.

SEE RELATED TOPICS
I'll be homesick: pp.22–23
I'm old enough to stay up late!: pp.42–43

HOW YOU COULD RESPOND

In the moment

Consider their development
Ask yourself: Have they stayed on their own with grandparents? Do they sleep well? Do they wet the bed? Would they say if they need something? Tell the host parents if your child is not ready, saying you will plan a sleepover in the future.

Find a compromise
You could suggest an evening playdate or "half-sleepover" in which they stay up later, and you pick them up just before bedtime.

Discuss how to be responsible
Talk about manners, like saying please and thank you, as well as respecting the host family's customs and rules. Get them to pack their own clothes, as well as anything they use to comfort themself at bedtimes.

Suggest a feast before midnight
Tweens often look forward to staying up later than they can cope with. Encourage them to have snacks for a "midnight" feast at an earlier hour.

Being a host
If you have agreed to host, lay down a set of reasonable rules so your child understands what is expected from them and their friends. This should include a time for lights out, how long they can chat afterward, how many treats they can have, and a no-internet rule in the bedroom. This will help them manage their guests' expectations from the outset—and they can blame any rules on you. As a host parent, expect to be on standby.

In the long term

Manage your own anxiety
Seeing your child go on a sleepover can be a departure for you too. View it as a step toward independence and show that you are confident in their ability to look after themself.

Confer with other parents
Communication between parents is important. Talk about times for drop-off, pick-up, and bedtime as well as food. Share your values on the internet and gadgets and tell

your child you have discussed it with the other child's family.

Take care
Check that any parental controls or internet filters are in place on gadgets, even if they do not use them in bedrooms. Tweens are more likely to visit sites they may not normally, including to pornographic websites. Older children may be tempted to show younger children images for the shock value.

SIBLING RELATIONSHIPS

Parents rank kids fighting with one another as the issue they find most difficult to deal with—and feel least able to prevent. Accepting it as a natural part of family life will help you cope.

Sibling rivalry stems from each child's primitive need to not miss out on their parents' care and protection, for their survival. Throw in the fact that squabbles will flare up because children haven't yet developed impulse control, and are learning to manage emotions such as frustration and jealousy, and conflict is inevitable. But as frustrating as the constant complaints and cries of "It's not fair" and "That's mine" can be, it helps to remember that all sibling rivalry is normal—and it can be helpful because it offers a safe training ground for children to learn how to deal with conflict.

1
Give one-to-one time
Children will fight over your attention. Head off concerns that other siblings get more of your time by having a dedicated period each day—even 10 minutes—when you are theirs. Staggered bedtimes are a way of having this special time.

4
Give each child space
Many sibling disagreements are about possessions: toys, clothes, gadgets. If it's not possible for each child to have their own room, give them a place to keep things they don't want to share.

7
Encourage empathy
Young tweens are still learning to see the world from other people's points of view. Help them extend their empathy by saying things like: "Your sister is sad today. Can we do anything to help her feel better?"

WORKING THINGS OUT

8 key principles

2

Accept angry feelings
As trivial as your kids' complaints may sound, listen to them. If they say a sibling called them a name, avoid saying: "Ignore it." Say: "Hearing your brother call you that must make you furious." Dismissing feelings leads to resentment. Show each child how to consider the other's point of view.

3

Acknowledge jealousy, too
Parents often feel they must instantly deny it when a child complains that "He's your favorite." Rather than gloss over jealousy, say you understand your child's feelings. Try something like: "I see that me spending more time with your brother while you are at baseball practice makes you angry." This way, they will feel heard.

5

Give time according to need
Your child will be hypervigilant about how much time they get with you. Explain why there may be periods when another child may need more time with you, like when they are ill. Remind them of times you did the same for them.

6

Model conflict resolution
Show how fighting and angry words never fix differences. In relationships with partners, relatives, and friends, show you can walk away when emotions get out of control, and come back and listen to what the other person has to say, state your own needs, and look for a way forward.

8

Notice what they do well
When siblings are sharing, or enjoying an activity together, make a point of acknowledging it. Say things like, "I see the way you have helped each other to make a new house for your action figures." It will make them more likely to repeat the behavior.

8–10 YEARS OLD

Encourage teamwork
Siblings will bond more if they have a common goal. Kids love board games and challenges at this age, so let siblings team up to try to beat the grown-ups.

Never compare
Children naturally compare themselves, so when you do it, they take it to heart. This is especially true if one child gets labeled "easy" and the other more "difficult." Avoid holding up a child's achievement in the hope it will encourage another.

10–12 YEARS OLD

Create safety
Watch out for a tween taking out frustration on younger siblings, who can be an easy target. Spend time with a tween who has lashed out—find the cause of their unhappiness and suggest ways to handle their anger. Ask them to tell you when they are about to lose their temper.

Value the relationship
Talk about how sibling relationships are likely to be the longest they ever have. While it's normal for siblings to annoy each other, they will always be an important support.

"I WANT A MAKEOVER PARTY"

As tweens become more curious about the steps older people take to present themselves to the adult world, they may be eager to experiment with makeup and beauty techniques to act and look older than they are.

SCENARIO | Your tween says they'd like a makeover party, at which they and their friends have manicures and experiment with makeup.

Many tweens are starting to use beauty and self-care products at an increasingly young age due to more marketing aimed at tweens. Some social media channels feature back-to-school makeup routines, and party companies offer makeovers for younger children. If your tween and their friends are aware of these activities, they are likely to want to try them. The messages your child takes from this will depend on the context you give it, and how much you help them to question the pressures on woman and men to look a certain way.

WHAT YOU MIGHT BE THINKING

You might think your child is too young to worry about looks, and fear being judged for throwing this party. Or, you might think it's harmless and fun.

SEE RELATED TOPICS
I need a bra: pp.102–103
I'm not pretty enough: pp.104–105

WHAT THEY MIGHT BE THINKING

◉ **Your tween may have seen how spa days and manicures** are a "treat" for people and want to try the experience as a way of feeling grown-up.

◉ **Now that your tween is thinking more about their future self**—and how they will look when they are older—they may want to experiment with gendered rituals like these, to see how they feel.

◉ **The beauty products themselves are appealing,** with different sensory textures, smells, and colors. Your tween will be curious about how using them makes them look and feel.

◉ **They may have received cultural messages** that wearing makeup and being pampered will make them feel admired, special, and confident.

HOW YOU COULD RESPOND

In the moment

Chat it through
Ask your child why they want this type of party. What will be fun about it? Where did they get the idea? Is it about feeling pampered or changing their appearance?

Make them aware
If they want to wear makeup, ask how it makes them feel and who it's for. Ask girls if they think the boys in their class would like to come too. If not, why? They may not know the answer, but it will encourage them to think about why girls focus on their appearance.

Keep it fun
Say while it's fun to change your appearance with makeup, for now it's a game for home, not for wearing outside, and they don't need to "improve" themselves.

Keep it creative
Suggest that they be made up to look like a favorite storybook character rather than a celebrity.

In the long term

Frame pampering as self-care
Make it clear there are other ways to feel good that have nothing to do with appearance, whether it's having a bubble bath or going for a walk to appreciate nature.

Question cultural norms
More than one-third of 7- to 10-year-old girls believe that women are judged more than men on their looks. Ask your tween why they think this is.

Be a role model
Show your tween that you feel comfortable both with makeup on, and without.

Emphasize choice
Say that if they wear makeup when they are older, it should be a choice, not an obligation.

Be aware of messaging
Let them enjoy the age they are. Avoid focussing on your child's looks, or predicting how they might look in the future.

Offer the bigger picture
Talk about how makeup advertising relies on consumers thinking they have problems to "fix" and are not good enough as they are.

> " "
> MAKE IT CLEAR THERE ARE OTHER WAYS TO FEEL GOOD THAT HAVE NOTHING TO DO WITH APPEARANCE.

"I GOT THE **BEST GRADE**"

At school, tweens are now being given more tests and grades for their work. As well as being ranked by adults, they are also starting to rank themselves against their peers and may start to relate this to their own self-worth.

SCENARIO | When you pick up your child from school, they tell you and everyone else nearby that they got the best grade in their spelling test.

We live in a competitive world in which parents get the message that their child must excel as soon as possible to do well in life. We also believe that telling them how good they are will encourage them to keep achieving. As children move up through the school system, they also increasingly measure their accomplishments against their classmates and notice that those who do well get rewarded with certificates and prizes. It's not surprising that they soon start to categorize each other into the "best" and the "worst." Over time, this may lead your child to think that they must win at everything—and let people know about it—in order to be seen as the success you want them to be.

WHAT YOU MIGHT BE THINKING

You may be thrilled and proud of your child's achievements but worried they are not taking others' feelings into account, and that their peers will see them as a show-off.

WHAT THEY MIGHT BE THINKING

◉ **Children are naturally curious when they start school,** but over time they can start to see all their achievements distilled into marks or grades and base their worth on these.

◉ **Your child may feel good when they tell others** they got the best grade, and enjoy winning your praise, not realizing that announcing their achievements can often make others feel like they are falling short.

◉ **If you often ask your tween what grade they got** and give your approval only when they do well, they may think they have to excel to earn your love.

◉ **Your child may have got the idea they need to beat others** to succeed, even though constant competition is stressful and can ruin friendships.

ASK WHAT INTERESTS THEM INSTEAD OF JUST FOCUSING ON RESULTS.

HOW YOU COULD RESPOND

In the moment

Acknowledge their intention
Your child wants you to be proud of them and to show how hard they have worked. Thank them for telling you and say something like: "You must feel good that your revision helped you do well in your spellings."

Point out the bigger picture
Help them see the value of learning by themself. You could point out: "Being able to spell well will help you write and express your ideas to other people more easily."

Encourage self-awareness
At a neutral time, help your tween to hear how they sound to others who are still developing those strengths. Talk about this in relation to your own wins and explain that while we want to inspire our peers and for everyone to succeed, we should be aware of the impact of telling others about our achievements.

In the long term

Notice their learning
If your child becomes hooked on being praised for getting the best grades in class, they may just see themself as the sum of their grades. Talk to them about what they are learning at school and what interests them instead of just focusing on results.

Value every quality
Encourage them to see themself as a well-rounded character who is more than just their achievements on paper. Ask what games they played, how they cooperated with others, or how their friendships are going.

Don't be overinvested
Adopt a tone of being interested but not intrusive so tweens don't think they have to excel to make you look good. Rather than fostering a winner-takes-all mentality, encourage your child to be a team player who values and praises the skills of others.

Check their schedule
If you have a high-achieving tween, hooked on academic rewards, make space in their days for downtime that's not about schoolwork. Look for opportunities for them to have fun, do nothing, explore, and get things wrong.

SEE RELATED TOPICS
They say I'm a show-off: pp.58–59
I'm scared I won't get a good grade: pp.138–139

"WE'RE BEST FRIENDS!"

From the age of around eight, your child may start seeking secure relationships outside the family and may choose a best friend. However, having a best friend can often come with strings attached.

SCENARIO | Your tween wants to have playdates and sleepovers only with their best friend.

As your child seeks stable relationships outside of your home, they may want to pair off with another schoolmate who they are proud to call their "best friend." When their best friend is around, your tween will feel protected against the unpredictability of school life. Tweens are likely to have high expectations of this bond, just as they will in romantic relationships later in life, and this high bar can lead to conflict. There are several ways to manage this when it occurs.

WHAT YOU MIGHT BE THINKING

You may be pleased your tween has a best friend so they always have someone to play with at break times. However, you may also worry that your child is sacrificing their individuality to mirror their friend.

◆ **SEE RELATED TOPICS** ◆
Can I go on a sleepover?: pp.82–83
I want a makeover party: pp.86–87

WHAT THEY MIGHT BE THINKING

◉ **Sharing interests with their friend will give them confidence** in their choices as your tween grows into their own person. To reinforce this, they may ask for matching clothes or accessories.

◉ **Sharing secrets is important in a best friendship**—this is probably the first time that your tween has revealed their thoughts to anyone outside of their family. They may ask for lots of playdates and sleepovers to build this intimacy.

◉ **Best friends often develop role-play games** that only they understand. This makes their friendship feel more special, but it may also mean they exclude others at playtimes.

◉ **If your tween feels their bestie is not loyal** or doesn't want to do all the same things, they may feel this breaks the invisible rules of "best friendship." Either best friend may threaten to withdraw the title to pressure the other to do what they want.

" "

SEE CONFLICT AS AN OPPORTUNITY FOR YOUR TWEEN TO DEVELOP IMPORTANT SKILLS, SUCH AS COMPROMISE.

HOW YOU COULD RESPOND

In the moment

Let them sort out conflict
Don't interfere—it's normal for best friends to have social conflict. See their friendship as an opportunity for your tween to develop social skills, such as negotiation, compromise, and maintaining boundaries. As best friends, they are likely to be very invested in making up after a disagreement, which allows them to practice these skills.

Discuss how friends don't need to be ranked
In best friendships, tweens can feel socially powerful. They may reinforce each other's negative views of certain classmates, making them act meanly. Talk to your tween about taking responsibility for their words and thinking about how others feel.

In the long term

Help them manage breakups
If their best friend moves on, your tween is likely to feel rejected. Teach them how to manage this shift by explaining that it's normal for friendships to come and go.

Keep social muscles strong
During a friendship breakup, give your child comfort, and remind them that after a period of hurt they will come out on the other side. Encourage them to find others to spend time with.

Remind them it's okay not to have a best friend
We live in a culture that romanticizes best friendship, which can make children feel like failures if they don't have a best friend of their own. As long as your child is not lonely, has a range of peers to be with most of the time, and enjoys school, that's enough. You could also read books together looking at how friendships can change over time.

"I'M A **LOSER**"

When they were younger, your child probably had no shortage of self-belief. Now, as a tween, they will begin to compare their skills with others and may feel frustrated and angry if they feel they are being left behind.

SCENARIO | When your tween is the only one struggling to keep up with their friends, they call themself a loser.

Feeling competent is important to your tween as they develop a sense of either industry, in which they feel they are "can-do" learners, or inferiority, where they feel "less than" others. The brain tends toward upward social comparison, meaning they compare themself to their peers with the greatest skills, not average or lesser ones. They may also compare themself with older peers, not realizing the difference a few months, and more practice, can make. On top of that, your tween may overgeneralize, saying they are not good at anything. While all children will say negative things—sometimes to vent feelings or preempt criticism—make sure negative self-talk doesn't become a habit.

WHAT YOU MIGHT BE THINKING

It may be upsetting to hear your tween making such a harsh generalization about themself. You may want them to be more resilient and wish they didn't take setbacks to heart.

◄ SEE RELATED TOPICS ►
I want to give up: pp.122–123
I'm so bad at sports: pp.142–143

WHAT THEY MIGHT BE THINKING

◉ **Your tween is using emotional thinking.** This means they feel this sense of disappointment in themself so strongly that it must therefore be the truth.

◉ **Putting themself down is your tween's way of saying** something negative before someone else does, which in turn protects them from expectations from others to do better.

◉ **They may not believe you if** you tell them they are not a loser, because your words don't match their feelings.

◉ **Your tween will be aware of social hierarchies,** and how being skilled—or not—affects their social standing. This means they will feel particularly sensitive to looking "like a loser" in front of their friends or other children their own age.

" "

SUGGEST THAT THEY TALK TO THEMSELF AS A KIND FRIEND OR GOOD COACH.

HOW YOU COULD RESPOND

In the moment

Listen
While it may be tempting to say, "Don't be silly—you're good at lots of things," acknowledge, rather than dismiss, their feelings. You could say: "I'm sorry you are feeling frustrated. Everyone finds things difficult at times, particularly at the beginning, but that doesn't make you a loser. It means you're still learning."

Dig deeper
Ask your child why they feel like this. Is it a throwaway line? Just a lighthearted comment, meant as a put-down before anyone else says it first? If you think your tween is being serious, ask more questions, such as: "What makes you say that?"

Change the focus
Explain that there are lots of ways to be clever, and we all have a unique combination. Suggest they name their top three skills, which are not comparison-based—perhaps being kind to animals, making others laugh, or baking.

In the long term

Name the inner critic
Your tween may think they have to listen to their inner critic, believing that it spurs them on to try harder. Explain that it helps only if it assists them in solving problems. Suggest that they talk to themself as a kind friend or good coach. Help them reframe their thinking.

Create characters
To help your tween realize they don't have to listen to their inner critic, help them imagine this dialogue coming from a character, which they could give a nickname to, such as Mr. Can't or Mrs. Negative. Tell them they are entitled to stand up to the character and argue back.

Encourage a growth mindset
If a tween can't do something, it's often because they haven't practiced enough yet. Acknowledge that learning is ongoing and that they will master most tasks eventually. Help them focus on things they can control—the effort they put in, rather than the outcome.

"I HATE YOU!"

When children are little and tell you "I love you,"
it feels like we are getting parenting right. So it can
be a shock to hear your older child saying words
such as "I hate you!"

SCENARIO | You ask your tween to stop watching their favorite movie because it's time for bed.

Tweens now feel more "grown up" and want more say over their lives. They are also developing theory of mind: the ability to imagine what other people are feeling. As they begin to understand the impact their words can have, they start testing boundaries. When they are looking forward to their favorite part of a movie, the levels of the feel-good chemical dopamine will be building in their brain's reward system. Interrupting this flow will trigger a stress response, which will surface as anger.

WHAT YOU MIGHT BE THINKING

When you have spent so many years loving your child, these words hurt. You may feel like you don't recognize them, may question your parenting skills, or may worry that this is the start of teenage behavior.

> **REMIND YOURSELF THAT YOUR TWEEN HATES BOUNDARIES; THEY DON'T HATE YOU.**

WHAT THEY MIGHT BE THINKING

⊙ **Your tween still loves you.** In that moment, they are interpreting their frustration as hatred. What they mean is, "I hate the fact you're not letting me do what I want."

⊙ **The word "hate" is a shortcut for the big feelings** they are struggling with in that moment. Remember that they are still developing the prefrontal cortex, which is the rational part of their brain.

⊙ **Your tween is trying to jolt you into changing your mind** by saying hurtful things. If your tween believes their angry outbursts have changed your mind before, they may think it's going to work again.

HOW YOU COULD RESPOND

In the moment

Don't take it personally
Remind yourself that your tween hates boundaries; they don't hate you. Your child's outburst is a sign that they trust you to keep loving them—it shows that they feel safe enough to express anger and are confident you won't reject them.

Defuse the situation
Your first instinct may be to say, "How dare you speak to me like that?" However, at this point your tween is not thinking logically, so demanding an apology will not help the situation.

Name the emotions
Use short sentences to name what they are feeling, without excusing their behavior, so they know you understand. You could say, "It's time to stop the movie. I understand you are feeling angry. We can talk about this later when everyone is calm."

Set a good example
One of the greatest skills you can model for your tween is emotional regulation. Briefly step away from the situation to stay in control of your feelings.

In the long term

Set consistent boundaries
If parents give in to children's demands, to protect them from disappointment or avoid a row, children can lash out when they don't get what they want. Stick to boundaries, and if you have a co-parent, stay on the same page.

Continue talking
Keep the lines of communication open so your tween can tell you how they are feeling at all times.

You could say, "Telling me you hate me shows me that you must have been feeling very upset. Please talk to me when you feel unhappy, so I can help you figure out how to manage that feeling."

Repair the relationship
When your tween has calmed down, spend special time together afterward to show you can go back to being close and loving again.

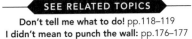

◄ **SEE RELATED TOPICS** ►
Don't tell me what to do! pp.118–119
I didn't mean to punch the wall: pp.176–177

"I DON'T WANT TO GO TO GRANDMA'S"

When your child was younger, there was no question that they'd go with you on family visits. Now that they are becoming more independent, your tween may be developing their own opinions on how they want to spend their time.

SCENARIO | Your child doesn't want to visit their grandparents because it's "boring." They want to play with a friend instead.

Grandparents can be trusted attachment figures who are the next best thing to parents. Studies show that grandparents can provide acceptance, patience, love, stability, and wisdom—and a close relationship can protect against future depression. A distance may open up if your tween does not see grandparents often or if their grandparents do not keep pace with your child's evolving interests.

WHAT YOU MIGHT BE THINKING

Your child's behavior may appear selfish. You may be worried that they will be moody during the visit and that their behavior will reflect on you.

WHAT THEY MIGHT BE THINKING

◉ **Tweens may feel grandparents treat them like babies,** and become bored at their house if grandparents do not keep up with the development stages your child is moving through.

◉ **They may resent feeling "forced" to go with you** out of a sense of family duty, if that's the message they are receiving. If you have a tricky relationship with your child's grandparents, your tween may have picked up on this and sense that the visits are a chore for everyone.

◉ **Your child may feel that they are missing out** if they can see what their friends are up to on messaging apps, or social media.

◉ **Your tween may resent having to abide by another set of rules** at another home, on food, screen time, and discipline. If you differ on strictness, your tween may not want to be stuck in the middle.

SEE RELATED TOPICS
I don't want to go to school: pp.108–109
I don't need a babysitter: pp.190–191

HOW YOU COULD RESPOND

In the moment

Empathize with your child
Acknowledge that going to their grandparents may not be their first choice of things to do but that families look out for one another and show their love in many ways, and one way is spending time together.

Involve your child
Use the travel time and period away from home to give your child some extra attention by playing games with them on the trip. Tell them how pleased you are that they are with you.

Role-model respect
Avoid giving the impression that visiting is a chore. Even if you and your parents have differences, role-model the kind of relationship you'd like to have with your children in the future.

In the long term

Reframe visits
Encourage your tween by suggesting they ask grandparents about family history or to share stories from your childhood. Before you arrive, suggest topics of interest that grandparents could bring up to connect with your child, or skills they could pass on.

Plan bonding time
If you live far away, tweens can often feel isolated and bored at a grandparent's house. Plan outings that the whole family can look forward to. Suggest some one-on-one time between each child and each grandparent so they can feel connected.

Maintain the relationship
Between visits, enable grandparents to keep in touch through video chats or via group chats where the whole family can swap pictures, jokes, and updates.

"THAT'S **BABYISH**"

Your tween's brain is starting to change as it matures.
Their changing interests and more sophisticated thinking
mean they may now view activities they loved just a few
months ago as "babyish."

SCENARIO | Your tween says they want to hide their cuddly toys away when their friends come over for a sleepover.

Your tween's brain is going through synaptogenesis—or growth of connections—which involves a pruning of the cells they are not using. Their brain is becoming more specialized and efficient. Now that they are more independent, tweens also view themselves as more "grown up" and may be eager to show how far they have come by distancing themselves from activities and games they used to love. However, toys still give tweens a sense of security and comfort, while role-playing with dolls, stuffed animals, or action figures is important for children this age to practice social skills and stretch their imaginations.

WHAT YOU MIGHT BE THINKING

You may feel sad your tween is leaving their childhood behind. You may be worried they are trying to act more grown up than they are, due to peer pressure.

WHAT THEY MIGHT BE THINKING

⊚ **As a young child, your tween talked to their dolls or animals** as if they were real. Their toy companions also made them feel more secure when you were not there. Now that your tween feels more grown up, they may start to feel embarrassed by their former dependence on them.

⊚ **Tweens who are slightly ahead of the curve developmentally** tend to hold more social power in groups. So your tween may be worried about being laughed at or put down by their friends for still having toys on display.

⊚ **Your tween may have figured out that calling another child's** activities or possessions "babyish" makes them sound more grown up and socially powerful.

⊚ **There will be moments when your tween acts like a teenager,** but at other times they may want to retreat to the safety of childhood, to the games and toys they used to play with. Development is not linear, and children can regress when they feel uncertain or insecure.

HOW YOU COULD RESPOND

In the moment

Reassure them
Understand your tween's need to belong and to impress their peers. Although you may worry they are hiding something they love for the sake of impressing friends, avoid making it a big deal and suggest they put their toys away in a cabinet temporarily so they can decide after the sleepover if they'd like them back.

Let them be their age
Your tween may still swing between activities they like now that they are older and ones they have always loved. Either way, avoid praising them for being "grown up" or shaming them for being "babyish."

Develop their interests
Make it clear that they don't have to leave their younger childhood behind. Suggest ways they can build on activities they have always loved. For instance, if they loved playing with dolls, they could now learn to sew clothes for them. Or if they loved playing with Lego bricks, they could try more sophisticated model-making.

In the long term

Talk about your toys
Tell them what your special toys meant to you, so they understand they don't need to feel ashamed of special possessions that are part of their life story.

Be playful
Look for other ways to play. Just because your tween wants to leave their childhood toys behind, don't leave them to play in the online world. Make play in different forms an ongoing part of family life. It reduces stress, creates memories, and draws you closer. If you are playful as a parent, then play will not be seen as something that only small children do.

Offer new ideas
Try activities like holding a friends-and-family sports day, with a water fight finale, or a board game or gaming tournament. Set aside time for activities to bridge childhood and adulthood, such as cooking, baking, doing crafts, or watching funny videos together.

SEE RELATED TOPICS

I'm old enough to stay up late: pp.42–43
I'll call you Dude, not Dad: pp.132–133

SEPARATION AND **DIVORCE**

For tweens, parental separation is a watershed moment. Hearing that their parents no longer want to be together is life-changing.

When parents separate, children have to get used to new homes and the absence of a person who made them feel safe. By the tween years, they will have clear ideas about how families "should" look. They will have memories of their old family life and may feel angry that these "rules" have been broken, without understanding the complexities of why splits happen. While research shows a family split is stressful for every child, parents can take steps to help them manage it. It's not the separation itself that is traumatizing; it's the conflict between parents. If you can keep your child's needs uppermost in your mind, they will cope better with the changes.

1
Tell them together
Agree with your co-parent how you will tell your child. Most children remember being told the news of their parents' separation for the rest of their lives. Come up with the words and speak to your child together in a positive, calm tone.

4
Be clear
Explain what's happening in terms of your child's life. Answer your child's main question: "Who's going to look after me?" Explain that you both will. You will just be living in different places.

7
Don't criticize your ex
Your ex is still your child's parent. Stay neutral or your tween will feel torn. Refer to each other by your parental names (e.g., Mommy) to show your roles will never change.

WORKING THINGS OUT

8 key principles

2

Set out the basics
Let the main message be: "Even though we are no longer living together, both of us will always be here to care for and love you." Rather than emphasize what will change, tell them what will stay the same.

3

See it from their perspective
While grown-ups see divorce for the complicated situation it is, tweens will see it in black and white. Avoid saying you no longer love each other, which makes love sound like a tap that can be switched off. Instead, explain that you have grown apart and you will live in two homes instead of one.

5

Help them be realistic
At this age, your child may fantasize about a reconciliation and wonder what they can do to make that happen. This can hold back their recovery and make it harder to accept new partners.

6

Listen to your tween
Your child may feel many different emotions, including anger. Let them know it's okay to feel all of them. Be prepared to give lots of comfort and reassurance.

8

Look after yourself
Ask family and friends for support or find groups. If you look after yourself, you will help your child more effectively. Use mediation services for negotiations if needed.

RATHER THAN EMPHASIZE WHAT WILL CHANGE, TELL THEM WHAT WILL STAY THE SAME.

! TAILORED ADVICE

8–10
YEARS OLD

Give comfort
Children often unload their feelings about difficult events by erupting over small triggers, such as losing a toy. Their grades at school could also suffer. Rather than see it as misbehavior, offer hugs and reassurance.

Educate them
Explain that there are many ways for families to be, and that not all children live with both of their parents.

Help them communicate
If your child is struggling to say how they feel, suggest they draw it or write a story, or you could read through books about divorce together.

10–12
YEARS OLD

Attend events together
A child should not have to choose which parent they want at events. Be polite and friendly to your former partner so your child can have you both there.

Form a united front
See your relationship with your co-parent as a business partnership. What's most important is the successful launch of your child. Put your feelings aside to make better decisions.

"I NEED A **BRA**"

For a tween girl, breast development is the most visible sign that she is in puberty. Your daughter may find some of these changes unsettling and need your reassurance to adjust to her changing body.

SCENARIO | Your tween comes home from school after a PE lesson and tells you she needs to start wearing a bra.

The first signs of breast development will be a feeling that there is a hard, coin-shaped mass growing under each nipple—these breast buds may feel tender. Next, the nipples and the areola around them will get larger, thicker, and darker. The nipples will then grow outward, making the breasts look pointy, before breast tissue grows underneath, giving the breasts a fuller shape. Welcoming the change and working with your tween to choose the right style and type of bra will help her feel positive about the changes, and will be a good introduction to a lifetime of wearing one.

WHAT YOU MIGHT BE THINKING

This may feel like a landmark moment to you—an official acknowledgement that your daughter is becoming more grown up. You may fear her being viewed in a more sexualized way before she is ready.

WHAT THEY MIGHT BE THINKING

⊙ **Even if your tween does not need a bra yet**, she may be feeling left out if her peers have started wearing them. She will feel more sensitive if she is an early or late developer compared to her friends.

⊙ **If your tween is developing bigger breasts** than her peers, she may wish it wasn't happening, want them to stop growing, or want a bra to make her development less obvious.

⊙ **Your tween may worry about her body changing** in ways she is not yet ready for if she has observed that breasts and bras are often sexualized by boys. Knowing she will probably have to wear a bra for the rest of her life may make her feel that her childhood is slipping away.

⊙ **Your tween may feel anxious and worried** about going bra shopping if she feels her breasts are growing at different rates, as many girls develop asymmetrically. If she's heard about cancer, she may also mistake the lumps made by breast buds for this, unless she asks a grown-up.

◄ **SEE RELATED TOPICS** ►
When will I get my period?: pp.148–149
They tease me about my boobs: pp.152–153

HOW YOU COULD RESPOND

In the moment

Be there and listen
While some tweens can't wait to have their first bra, others will feel embarrassed at broaching the subject. Take your child's request seriously, even if you are not sure she needs a bra yet.

Be curious
To get the best bra for your tween, chat about the main reasons she wants one. Is it because she feels self-conscious that her breasts are showing through her clothes? Does she feel left out without one? Are her breasts getting in the way when she runs, jumps, or does sports?

Search together
If your tween is comfortable, set aside some time to search for the styles that work for her stage of development. Depending on how she feels, offer to take her shopping, or look online together if she is more self-conscious.

Get a proper fitting
If your tween has already developed larger breasts, take her to be measured professionally. Take her cues as to how much privacy she wants in her changing room. Look for soft cotton or bamboo bras, rather than underwired ones, unless she needs the support. Explain if a bra fits well and is properly adjusted, she shouldn't feel it. Tell her to keep you up-to-date about when she might have outgrown it to send the message bras should fit well and be comfortable.

In the long term

Demystify breast development
Explain that female sex hormones are sending messages to her body to grow in new ways. Make it clear that breast development is part of a gradual process that will allow her to breastfeed a baby if she chooses to, but that's a long time in the future. For now, she is still a child, these changes are natural, and she doesn't need to hide her breasts by hunching over, crossing her arms, or wearing baggy clothes.

Talk about real breasts
Breasts are portrayed in the media as uniformly round, high, and perky. Point out that breasts do, in fact, come in different shapes and sizes and there is no "right" way for them to look. If your daughter's breasts are growing at different rates, reassure her they will even out, but breasts are never 100 percent symmetrical.

"I'M NOT **PRETTY ENOUGH**"

As tweens become more aware of how others view them, and observe classmates and friends who are conventionally attractive having more social power, they may start to fret about how their looks compare.

SCENARIO | On the way home from school, your daughter tells you she's doesn't think she's as pretty as her friends.

As part of wanting to fit in with their social group, your tween may start to compare their appearance to others. At the same time, they will be taking more notice of cultural stereotypes of what it means to be "pretty." While this worry will be hard to hear, your tween is at a stage when they are open and receptive to what you have to say. So this is an ideal time to explain that these feelings will always come and go, but what will not change is their intrinsic worth.

WHAT YOU MIGHT BE THINKING

You may be shocked to hear your child say something so mean about themselves and want to immediately reassure them they are beautiful, to make you both feel better.

WHAT THEY MIGHT BE THINKING

◉ **Until they discover that many things make someone attractive**, such as style, character, humor, and originality, tweens may be impressed by peers whose looks conform to ideals in the media.

◉ **Girls tend to get more praise for looks than boys**, who get complimented more on strength and assertiveness. It can mean girls grow up thinking their appearance is the most important thing about them and that being pretty pleases others. They are also more likely than boys to believe they "are" their looks.

◉ **If your tween has heard you criticize your own looks** or pass judgment on others, they may have internalized this negative voice and turned it on themself.

◉ **Your tween may be seeking reassurance.** But even when you tell them they are beautiful, they may dismiss it, thinking you are only saying it because you are their parent.

SEE RELATED TOPICS
I want a makeover party: pp.86–87
Why can't I wear mascara to school?: pp.184–185

HOW YOU COULD RESPOND

In the moment

Offer a hug
Give comfort as you help them understand. Rather than deny or contradict, ask, "What is making you feel this way?" Explore whether they are worried about something else, such as being rejected by their peers.

Listen
Tweens don't want to disappoint their parents, so this is a painful subject to raise. Thank them for communicating their feelings, as this will help them feel capable and special in a different way.

Reflect back
Summarize their concerns so they know you have understood. Say, "It sounds like you feel that …" Allowing your tween to share in this way, and showing you have understood, will reduce the power of painful feelings.

Offer perspective
Normalize their feelings and reassure them lots of people worry about appearance. Mention there are likely to be many people who admire them for their strengths.

In the long term

Change your messaging
Make it a family value that appearance is never the most important thing. Acknowledge what your tween does, by complimenting them on kindness, humor, and honesty, which are more in their control than looks.

Name the inner critic
Make your tween aware of the critical voice in their head. The voice can act like a bully. It's okay to disagree and argue back because what they are hearing are thoughts, not facts.

Tackle the worry cycle
Your tween may get caught in repetitive thought loops, such as,

"I won't be happy unless I look pretty." Help them notice these limiting beliefs and their effect. Offer them a circuit breaker thought, such as, "My body is a gift," or suggest an activity that turns their focus outward and makes them feel better.

Be a positive role model
Refrain from criticizing your own appearance, talking about diet, or weighing yourself in front of your tween. Encourage your child to question a culture that makes people feel like their worth is based on how they look.

REFRAIN FROM CRITICIZING YOUR OWN APPEARANCE IN FRONT OF YOUR TWEEN.

CHAPTER 2

YOUR
10 – 12
YEAR-OLD

"I DON'T WANT TO GO TO SCHOOL"

Most children will have the odd day when they don't want to go to school, but if it starts to become a pattern, you will need to act quickly to uncover the underlying issues.

SCENARIO | Your tween is getting into a habit of refusing to get out of bed to get ready for school.

Tweens know it's their "job" to go to school and learn. When they try to avoid school, it's important to find out why. Some reasons are short-term, such as tiredness, a friendship flare-up, fear they will be picked on, or concerns about doing badly on a test. Longer-term issues may be social anxiety—a fear of being judged by their peers—or separation anxiety—a fear of being apart from you. They may also be having difficulties with learning or social skills, making them feel so disheartened, overwhelmed, or anxious that they can't face going. Whatever the reason, school avoidance is often a tween's last resort to express how unhappy they feel.

WHAT YOU MIGHT BE THINKING

You may feel powerless as you can't force your child to go to school, and you may be worried about the adverse effects it may have on their learning.

WHAT THEY MIGHT BE THINKING

◉ **If you insist they go to school, without trying to connect** with them and find out why, your tween may react in a number of ways, ranging from becoming angry and lashing out to lying in bed in silence because they are too low to express how they feel.

◉ **If they are anxious, they may feel physically unwell** with a headache or stomach pains, for example, as children's bodies are sensitive to emotions.

◉ **They may feel they have hit a brick wall** and that's why it is coming to a head now. Your tween's school avoidance can seem sudden, but it can surface when they feel no longer able to mask their feelings of anxiety or being overwhelmed.

◉ **Staying at home may feel like the safest option** if your child is feeling anxious, but the temporary relief may encourage them to avoid school next time they feel they can't cope, so refusing to go to school may happen more often.

SEE RELATED TOPICS
I want to give up: pp.122–123
My teacher hates me!: pp.146–147

HOW YOU COULD RESPOND

In the moment

Take your time
Take the pressure off yourself so you can react more calmly. Call the school and tell them you are dealing with a delay at home. If you are expected at work, tell colleagues you have a personal issue to deal with. If your tween continues to refuse, arrange a flexible working day or ask a family or friend to stay with them.

Make a connection
Rather than threaten, or call your child lazy, meet them where they are. Let them know you're there to hear why it's difficult. Ask no-judgmental questions such as, "What's stopping you from feeling like going to school today?" and "What can I do to help?" Show them you are ready to listen.

Be a detective
Many tweens find it difficult to articulate their reasons, so try and zone in by asking questions about aspects of school: "How much do you like break times?" "How much do you enjoy lessons?" and "How much do you like your teacher?" on a scale of 1–10.

Make home boring
Remove any leisure activities, such as video games and TV, which can make home feel like a better alternative to school.

In the long term

Talk about coping
If you suspect this is a one-off that will pass, use "brave talk" to tell your child you believe they can get through the school day. Recall challenges they have overcome. When your child does go to school, listen to how it went. Reflect back on any difficult feelings instead of trying to put a positive spin on things.

Find solutions
If they keep avoiding school, they will need help to see it as manageable again. Do they need support with any subjects? Are they struggling to make friends? If they are in trouble with a teacher, could they explain why they are behaving a certain way? Talk about problem-solving ideas.

Act soon
If your tween is slipping into a pattern, don't hide it from the school, or it can snowball. Take a collaborative approach with your child and their teacher. This could include looking into any learning or sensory challenges, adjusting their timetable, or having a staff member greet your child to help them settle.

"I'M **GOING TO BE FAMOUS** WHEN I GROW UP"

To a tween, celebrities and influencers seem to have it all: popularity, status, and wealth. As social media makes fame look easy, some tweens may believe that "being famous" is a legitimate career goal in its own right.

SCENARIO | Your tween loves filming themself and says when they grow up, they are going to be a famous YouTuber.

By now your tween is becoming more aware of life outside their family and is thinking about what their future might look like. Beyond this, they are observing that we live in a culture that admires celebrities and gives them a high status. Furthermore, social media makes getting attention look easier and more within reach than ever. The result is that more children are putting professions such as "influencer" and "celebrity" at the top of the list of jobs they would like to do when they grow up.

WHAT YOU MIGHT BE THINKING

You might be wondering what happened to conventional job aspirations and worry that your tween won't try at school if they believe they can become famous by posting on social media.

WHAT THEY MIGHT BE THINKING

- **If your tween is already posting on social media,** and getting social status from receiving a lot of comments and likes, it may not seem like a big leap from doing this to becoming "famous."

- **They may believe wealth and fame can be achieved overnight,** rather than from hard work and skill. They may have observed a culture where people have gained instant celebrity thanks to reality TV shows and social media.

- **Your tween sees only the plus sides of fame**: being rich, popular, and admired. They haven't yet developed the critical capacity to think about the downsides.

- **Influencers can have a bigger effect on tweens** than parents realize. If your tween shares common interests, and follows certain online personalities every day, they may feel like they "know them" and are like them. This may lead them to believe that fame is in easy reach for them too.

◆ **SEE RELATED TOPICS** ▶
Why can't I go on TikTok?: pp.124–125
My selfie got 100 likes!: pp.140–141

HOW YOU COULD RESPOND

In the moment

Talk about the reality
While it's fine for your tween to experiment with this idea at this phase of identity development, at other times, help them consider the reality behind being an influencer. Chat about the pros and cons. While money and status might seem to be on the plus side, what pressures are people under to keep supplying material to feed the algorithm and stay popular? What hurdles have established celebrities faced to get to the top of their professions?

Be curious
While it's tempting to suggest your tween considers more serious career goals, ask questions so they start thinking realistically. Do they foresee their fame as being based on a skill or an achievement? If they plan to become an influencer, what do they intend to specialize in? How will they stand out?

In the long term

Offer perspective
Point out how the social media influencers and celebrities who come up most often on social media feeds—and make a living from it—represent only a tiny percentage of the hundreds of thousands of people trying to get noticed.

Encourage self-awareness
Help your tween ask questions about the online world. If they post, do they feel disappointed if a picture gets only a few likes? Does social media feel like a competition? Chat about how this is the reality for many online celebrities, only on a much bigger scale, because once they are well known, it can become a battle to retain their popularity and relevance.

Help them feel important
If your tween seems to want a lot of online admiration, invite them to spend more time with you and other people close to them in the real world doing activities that make them feel capable. Help them notice and be grateful for what is already good about their lives.

Explore positive role models
Ask who they follow on social media and why. Help them find role models in the wider world, like environmentalists, scientists, and entrepreneurs. Also talk about people you know personally who make the world a better place with kindness and hard work. Talk about the difference between fame and worth, and how they are not the same thing.

PUBERTY

If there is one question that pops up a lot in a child's mind as they go through puberty, it's "Am I normal?" At times, seeing their bodies change will be scary and embarrassing for them.

The age of the onset of puberty is falling for both boys and girls worldwide, possibly due to changes in food and the environment. It may help to see puberty as a cascade of hormonal changes that start as early as seven or eight, before you spot the first signs in your child. Another reason to start the conversation early is that kids can now see information on sex and puberty from many sources. If they don't hear it from you, they may go to unsuitable or ill-informed places on the internet to look for answers. Be there to listen and provide a balanced, caring perspective so they don't feel alone with their body's changes or confused by what they see or hear.

1

Explain hormones
Let them know that their brains and glands send out chemical messages and that these tell different parts of their body to change gradually. These changes happen to everyone so that they will grow into adults and have the choice about whether to have children.

> " "
> EVEN THOUGH THE TIMING IS OUT OF THEIR CONTROL, THEY HAVE A CHOICE ABOUT HOW TO DEAL WITH THE SHIFTS.

WORKING THINGS OUT

6 key principles

2
Say timings will vary
Talk about how even if their friends are the same age, they may show signs of puberty at different times and nothing can change the speed. Help empower them by explaining they still have choices about how to deal with these shifts, like when to get a bra or seek out a relationship.

3
Talk about the brain
Tell them that rising levels of the female sex hormone estrogen in girls and the male sex hormone testosterone in boys affects their brains. They may be able to tell when hormones are circulating because they may feel more emotional for a while and start to feel attracted to others in new ways.

4
Look for opportunities
It's normal to feel uncomfortable talking about puberty with your child. Look for age-appropriate educational videos you can watch together to launch the talk. Have a two-way conversation where they ask questions. Suggest they can write questions in a shared notebook, where you can respond.

5
Describe it as a journey
Explain that puberty is a long phase, lasting at least five years, when their bodies will slowly change. Tell your tween how it will be a continuation of the growth they have gone through since they were babies and reassure them they will always be the same person on the inside.

6
Be positive
While boys tend to look forward to puberty because it gives them strength and autonomy, girls tend to dread it, fearing periods and judgment for their appearance. Be positive for girls too. Focus on advantages, like getting taller and having more independence. Ask your daughter if she would like to celebrate when her first period arrives.

! TAILORED ADVICE

8–10 YEARS OLD

Think about timings
If you raise the topic early, before your tween becomes self-conscious about their bodies, they may be more receptive.

Give reassurance
Tell girls period blood isn't the same as getting cut: it builds up the lining of the womb for potential babies. Explain to boys that voices don't "break." They deepen as vocal cords thicken.

Offer books
Tweens need time to process it all. Offer warm, authoritative books they can digest in their own time.

10-12 YEARS OLD

Don't give up
Even if they dismiss this as "yucky," the information is going in. Say it will make sense when they are older.

Use the third person
Take the focus off them by asking if any of their friends have started their period or have a voice that has broken. Assure them you will keep chats confidential.

Make nothing off limits
Make it clear you are happy to talk about anything. If asked about masturbation, acknowledge it feels good and is not harmful but is always done in private.

"THEY POSTED A **MEAN MESSAGE**"

While social media offers many ways for tweens to interact, it also provides more opportunities for them to get into social conflict. It's important for you to be aware of the risks and encourage open communication with your child.

SCENARIO | Your tween is upset because a classmate posted a meme in their WhatsApp group making fun of their appearance.

As your tween starts to use social media, outbreaks of conflict become likely. From behind a screen, they are more likely to post images or make comments they would not say face-to-face because they can't see a reaction, particularly as there are no grown-ups around. They may be tempted to make comments or post pictures to entertain others, and social media moves so fast they will act without thinking. Conflict online can take many forms, from comments in group chats to sharing unflattering photos and passive-aggressive memes.

WHAT YOU MIGHT BE THINKING

You may feel shocked at the meanness, sad for your child, regretful that you allowed them to join social media, and so angry you want to get in touch with the parents of the other child.

► SEE RELATED TOPICS ◄
They're teasing me: pp.40–41
They didn't save me a seat at lunchtime: pp.72–73

WHAT THEY MIGHT BE THINKING

⊚ **Your tween may fear telling you.** If your response is that they are not old enough to be on social media, they will be concerned that you will take their device away.

⊚ **Your tween is likely to be anxious about how many** peers have seen the post and may feel worried about going to school the next day.

⊚ **They will want the whole drama to just go away** and will be scared you will complain to the offending child's parents and make it worse.

⊚ **They may be hurt by peers who witness it and say nothing** in their defense, often because they are afraid the person who posted the mean message will turn on them too.

HOW YOU COULD RESPOND

In the moment

Offer a hug
If they want support, you could say something like: "People say things they don't mean on social media so they look funny or powerful. What they did was unkind. We can't take away the message, but you can chat to your friends to feel better."

Avoid removing their device
Although you may think you are saving them from more upset, they will become more anxious if they can't monitor what's being said about them and will avoid telling you if it happens again. They will also want to stay in touch with friends who may help them feel better.

Encourage brainstorming
Instead of intervening, offer to help them come up with their next move. They might ignore the post, respond with humor, or ask the poster to remove it. They could also take screen grabs in case it escalates.

In the long term

Provide context
Talk to your tween about how conflict is a normal part of human interaction and everyone experiences it. Many of these outbreaks will take place among groups of friends and are "relational aggression"—or status power plays—rather than bullying. Unless mean posts and comments are targeted, repeated, and intended to cause deliberate hurt toward a socially less powerful person who can't fight back, one cruel message is likely to be manageable. If it continues, you may have to help your child move on to a new friendship group.

Stay close
Expect mistakes during the tween years as your child learns the ropes. Try to see blow-ups as opportunities for them to learn lessons rather than swooping in to defend them. Keep talking to them about their online lives.

"NOTHING! IT WAS JUST A NORMAL DAY"

Once, your child couldn't wait to tell you everything they did at school when they got home. So when they start not wanting to talk about their day, you may feel shut out or even worried.

SCENARIO | Your tween seems in a bad mood at dinner, but when you ask them what happened at school, they say, "Nothing. It was just a normal day."

Your child is going through a period of transition. They are becoming more inwardly focused and turning more toward relationships with their peers, who they may believe understand them better. At the same time, they are learning that they don't have to tell you everything. School lessons are also becoming more demanding and tiring. All of this means that your tween may no longer be as chatty and as eager to fill you in on their day as they once were. However, meet them where they are and look for new ways to communicate so you are connected in readiness for the teenage years.

WHAT YOU MIGHT BE THINKING

You may miss your little chatterbox and wonder whether there is something you should know. You might feel rejected if they are messaging friends.

WHAT THEY MIGHT BE THINKING

⊚ **Your tween has had to behave, concentrate, abide** by adult rules, and spend time with classmates they didn't choose all day. Their social and mental batteries are now running low, so they need time to recharge and decompress.

⊚ **They have figured out that you don't know everything** just because you are their parent, so they are becoming more selective about what they share with you.

⊚ **Their day will have involved spending time with friends** and sharing experiences and secrets with them. They won't want to recap on the whole day because they think that, as a grown-up, you wouldn't understand anyway.

⊚ **If something is bothering them, they may fear that** you might overreact or want to get involved, or lecture or criticize them, especially if you've jumped in before to give advice instead of really listening and empathizing with them.

HOW YOU COULD RESPOND

In the moment

Avoid taking it personally
Rather than nag your tween, see this separation as a healthy part of their development as they start to become an individual with their own private thoughts and feelings. For now, it will help to adjust your expectations of how much your tween wants to tell you.

Listen
As a parent, you are used to doing a lot of the talking. To encourage your child to open up, listen more than you talk, and don't jump in, interrupt, or pass judgment. Also avoid trying to "fix" any feelings or issues your tween may be having. When they want to chat, be curious without interrogating. Feel for them, while having some simple phrases ready to show that you are listening, such as, "What was that like for you?" and "That sounds tough."

In the long term

Wait until later
Find another time to synchronize. Let your tween have some downtime and, without adding pressure, see if there are other ways to connect later, whether it's sharing a snack and drink, cooking together, playing a game, or having a chat at bedtime.

Tune in to boys
Boys have a reputation for being more "silent" when, in fact, they have been socialized to believe that expressing feelings is not manly. Look for cues they want to chat, like hovering around you for no reason, and try to find activities and opportunities to just "be" together.

Help them find the words
Studies show that children are better at expressing emotions when they have been shown how to describe them by adults. Name your own feelings as you feel them and help your tween to identify their own.

Offer another confidante
If your child persists in shutting you out and you are starting to worry, remember it's fine to seek help from another family member or a professional. Avoid allowing your child to ruminate alone in their bedroom for long periods, especially on social media.

SEE RELATED TOPICS
I don't want to go to school: pp.108–109
I am telling the truth: pp.166–167

"DON'T TELL ME WHAT TO DO!"

Your tween is transforming from a child who has had most things decided for them into an adolescent who believes they know best. They may resent being told what to do if they feel you are not recognizing their burgeoning independence.

SCENARIO | When you question your tween's casual outfit choice for a wedding, they say they "know" what to wear to weddings and this is perfect.

As they have moved from early childhood to adolescence, your tween has learned a lot in a few years. As tweens have a logical style of thinking, they tend toward an oversimplified view of life. Until they start to move into a more sophisticated, abstract style of thinking, known as "Formal Operational," around age 12, and start understanding other people's perspectives, tweens can seem very certain about everything. This can come across as bossiness and a know-it-all attitude.

WHAT YOU MIGHT BE THINKING

It may amuse you that your tween is an "expert" on everything, although their bossiness may annoy you. Plus, you may worry the outfit they picked will reflect badly on you.

SEE RELATED TOPICS
You can't tell me what to eat!: pp.182–183
It's not my job: pp.186–187

WHAT THEY MIGHT BE THINKING

◉ **Tweens tend to believe what parents tell them** about who they are. If you have often praised your child and told them how grown-up, smart, or stylish they are, they may now believe they know it all.

◉ **It is common for tweens to be black-and-white thinkers** and some may be inflexible after they have made up their mind.

◉ **Your tween may have a more patronizing tone** if they are the eldest sibling and are used to being in charge.

◉ **Tweens now have improved memories** and may be able to remember more facts in a short time than adults. This may lead them to believe that they know more than you about everything—and want to show off about this.

" "

HELP THEM CHANNEL ASSERTIVENESS BY GIVING THEM MORE CONTROL IN CERTAIN AREAS, SUCH AS HELPING PLAN A TRIP OR A SPECIAL MEAL.

HOW YOU COULD RESPOND

In the moment

Ask them to try again
You could say something like, "I know it feels good to feel certain, but your tone makes it hard for me to hear your point of view at the moment."

Encourage wider thinking
Help them consider other perspectives. You could say something like, "I also have experience of going to weddings, which are special events with dress codes. So when you're ready, I'd also like to share my perspective and then we can decide together."

Remember it's a phase
While it may be annoying now, bear in mind that it won't be long before your child starts to see the world in a more nuanced way—and self-doubt and self-consciousness starts to creep in. Until that happens, you don't have to address every issue—let them enjoy this self-confident phase.

In the long term

Channel their assertiveness
Being assertive is a positive quality, as long as they can consider the views of others and communicate skillfully. Give them an outlet for it by offering more control in other areas, such as helping plan a family trip or a special meal.

Check your tone
If you often use an overbearing tone of voice, your tween may be copying you. Speak to them, and others, in a way in which you would like to be spoken to.

Let them learn
Parents tend to want to save tweens from embarrassment or hurt. But if your tween is making a decision that will not have any long-lasting negative effect on their own lives or others, let them experiment. They will make better decisions, and learn more resilience, if they learn for themselves.

STARTING
MIDDLE SCHOOL

When your child starts middle school, it may feel like the first part of their childhood is coming to an end.

It will also be a big shift for your tween, who will have to adjust to longer days, more subjects, new friends, and bigger class sizes. Middle school will bring new decisions for you to make, including whether to let your child travel to school on their own or to have a cell phone. Whatever challenges school brings, tweens who can talk to their parents will be happier and fare better. Even if they don't want to share everything that happened during the day, be a comforting presence who is there to listen if they want to offload, and create a home where they can unwind.

1
Dispel any myths
Kids may have heard scary stories from older kids about detentions, bullying, getting lost on the way to class, and mean teachers. Ask what they've heard and talk through the realities so your child feels ready and reassured.

4
Talk about making friends
Discuss how to get off to a good start. Suggest icebreakers: smiling, saying hello, and asking questions such as how others spent their summer. Explain that basic courtesy gives them an advantage. Remind them everyone is nervous and looking for friends. If they had social difficulties in elementary school, offer practice building these skills.

7
Encourage clubs
Joining a club allows them to develop a talent to make them feel special. It will also expose them to a wider range of potential friends.

WORKING THINGS OUT

7 key principles

2

Explain the differences
They may be going from a small classroom with one class teacher to larger classrooms with many teachers who don't yet know who they are. Prepare them for this change and tell them the bottom line is that it will always help to listen, be polite, and ask questions if they don't understand.

3

Give run-throughs
Offer to practice in any areas they feel would help. Attend school open days and do trial runs of the trip. Show them how to use a planner and the padlock they'll need for their locker. Visit the school website with them and take advantage of any maps or virtual tours so that your child feels less overwhelmed.

5

Expect friendship challenges
Help them understand they don't have to be popular to be socially successful and that friendship comes in many shapes. Tell them some social conflict is normal but that assertive, kind communication can dial down drama.

6

Consider an assessment
Some children will have started to give up if they didn't feel good enough at elementary school. If your child's confidence has been dented, and if they had trouble keeping up, ask now for an educational assessment. Any issues are likely to be amplified in middle school.

> **" "**
>
> PREPARE THEM FOR THIS CHANGE AND TELL THEM IT WILL ALWAYS HELP TO LISTEN, BE POLITE, AND ASK QUESTIONS IF THEY DON'T UNDERSTAND.

TAILORED ADVICE

10–12
YEARS OLD

Set homework habits
Homework will now increase. Set aside a spot at home, make a rule that there is no video game or phone use until homework is done, and encourage your child to use a timer to stick to the allotted time for tasks, so they stay focused and have time to relax after school.

Be organized
Middle school requires far more organization from both you and your tween. Create a hub in the kitchen to post a daily checklist for items they need to take in, a timetable, and a folder for school paperwork.

Offer playdates
It will help your tween to have friends who are outside the intense microcosm of classroom politics. If your tween has elementary school friends they want to stay in touch with, encourage meet-ups.

Play "What if?"
They will adjust better if they know they can cope when things don't go to plan. Play "What if?" so they can think what to do if they forget their PE clothes, lose their bus pass, or get a detention. Let them ask you questions, too, to hear how you handle challenges.

"I WANT TO **GIVE UP**"

It can be disappointing when, after months or years
of lessons and practice, your tween says they no longer
want to carry on with extracurricular activities, such
as playing a musical instrument.

SCENARIO | After two years of playing the violin, your tween
tells you they want to give up lessons.

Many parents sign up children for music lessons
because it's good for their brain development
and concentration and because they want to see if
they have musical talent. However, as tweens try to
figure out their place in the world, they increasingly
judge themselves in relation to others. Due to the
human tendency for "upward comparison,"
they compare themselves to the best musician
in their peer group. This can leave them feeling
inadequate and disheartened—but the good
news is that you can help them gain
perspective on their progress.

WHAT YOU MIGHT BE THINKING

**You may think your tween is
giving up too easily** and should
persevere until they reap the
benefits, such as music grades or
improved concentration. You may
feel you have wasted time and
money on lessons.

SEE RELATED TOPICS
I'm a loser: pp.92–93
My teacher hates me: pp.146–147

WHAT THEY MIGHT BE THINKING

⊚ **Tweens are prone to all-or-
nothing thinking.** If they feel they
don't have time to perfect their
pieces, or are not the best violin
player in their school year, they
may want to give up altogether.

⊚ **They might want to try other
activities.** When they were
younger, your tween wouldn't
have had much choice about
extracurricular activities. They
are now developing their sense
of self and an understanding of
their aptitudes and interests.

⊚ **They feel they have enough
to do.** Your tween has more
commitments now and could be
finding rehearsals and practice
time-consuming. This may also
mean they miss out on time with
friends at breaks and after school.

⊚ **Your tween may not like their
music teacher.** They may hate
practicing alone, or the criticism
that comes if they don't play well.
They may feel like music lessons
are an extra pressure to achieve
that they can do without.

HOW YOU COULD RESPOND

In the moment

Hear them out
Listen to their reasons for wanting to give up and summarize them without judgment, so they feel heard. Talking through how they feel may help them think clearly.

Talk through alternatives
Is this a temporary feeling that could be fixed by changing teachers or learning new pieces? Do they hate missing break times, or are they missing classes to go to music lessons and falling behind with schoolwork? See if they would like to brainstorm ways to make lessons more enjoyable.

Find out if practice is a problem
If they are getting in trouble for not practicing their instrument or skill enough, try a new approach. For example, 10 minutes a day of "snack" practice is better than one long session each week, and it often reaps better results.

Remind them of their progress
It's easy for tweens to take what they have learned for granted. Could they still make the most of their musical progress by switching to an instrument better suited to their personality?

In the long term

Teach honoring commitments
If you agree with them that they can drop the activity, ask them to wait until the end of the term or their current lesson cycle, to reinforce the importance of honoring their commitments.

Tone down competition
Your tween may feel that excelling in their extracurricular activity has become more important to you than it is to them. Tell them that if they enjoy playing an instrument, that's reason enough to keep doing it, as playing and listening to music is a great way to relax and express feelings. It shouldn't feel like a competition, or a race to

achieve grades. You could explain that adults who gave up learning an instrument often regretted it later.

Find their spark
Tweens need to feel that they are "good" at something. If their current activity is no longer bringing them joy, help them figure out their "spark"—the activity they are naturally drawn to and would do even if they were not asked. They are far more likely to stick to an extracurricular activity based on their innate strengths.

> " "
> THEY ARE FAR MORE LIKELY TO STICK TO AN ACTIVITY BASED ON THEIR STRENGTHS.

"WHY CAN'T I GO ON **TIKTOK?**"

By now, your child probably knows other kids their age who have been allowed to sign up to social networks, even though the age limit is 13. If your tween asks to do the same, you are likely to feel torn.

SCENARIO | Your child is angry that you won't let them sign up for TikTok because they have not yet reached age 13.

Kids see grown-ups using social networks and, like us, want to post pictures and connect with friends. According to an Ofcom report, 6 out of 10 tweens are already on social media; parents often allow them to lie about their age. But your tween doesn't yet have the perspective to understand why they are not ready. From the age of eight, kids become more aware of risks but still tend to overestimate their ability to deal with them. Allowing them to sign up at a young age is a health and well-being issue.

WHAT YOU MIGHT BE THINKING

You are likely to be worried they are too naïve to handle what can happen online and concerned about what message you are giving them if you allow them to lie about their age.

WHAT THEY MIGHT BE THINKING

⊙ **If just a couple of their friends** have been allowed to sign up to social media, in your tween's mind, that is "everybody."

⊙ **Even if you explain the risks**, your tween will insist they would never be so "silly" as to fall for them because they believe they already know everything.

⊙ **If you have previously given in to your child** by buying video games recommended for players over their age, your tween may secretly believe they can wear you down.

⊙ **If they are affected by FOMO**—an intense fear of being left out of the jokes, games, and chats they think their friends are sharing without them—it will cause them to panic and continually nag you.

" "
BE A ROLE MODEL: TALK ABOUT HOW YOU LIMIT YOUR SOCIAL MEDIA USE, TOO.

SEE RELATED TOPICS

All my friends have a phone: pp.62–63
I'm going to be famous when I grow up:
pp.110–111

HOW YOU COULD RESPOND

In the moment

Stick to boundaries
Explain to your tween that their brain is still developing and that social media is designed to be super-stimulating. Tell them it's too early for them to be distracted from the fun real-world things they love: playdates, being outside, arts and crafts, which are important for them to feel good. You could say: "While you are still growing, your social life should be happening in the real world."

Consider their development
Tweens do not yet have the life experience to view what they see in perspective. For example, if your child tends to be impulsive, or has a lot of friendship dramas in real life, this is likely to be amplified on social media. Experts agree it's better to hold the line as long as possible.

Get a reality check
Research shows that kids' social lives don't suffer without social media until they reach secondary school. Before that, being online may hinder rather than help. This is because tweens, who are still developing impulse control and empathy, tend to have more fallouts. Cyberbullying peaks around the age of 12—a year before children are supposed to be on social networks.

In the long term

Give them practice
Consider letting them try one platform, like a closed group of friends on WhatsApp, for a limited time. If all goes well, suggest you will consider allowing them to sign up to social media when they start secondary school.

Monitor usage
In the same way a driving instructor has dual controls, it's fine to accompany your child when they have their first messaging account, whether it's by sharing passwords or monitoring their usage.

Keep it public
Say they can use social media only on devices that belong to the whole family, such as a tablet, which stay in common areas. Keep these out of bedrooms. Sexting and grooming mostly starts when adults are not present.

Be a role model
Role model how even you, as an adult, take precautions, whether it's blocking strangers or asking questions about links you are sent. Talk about how you limit your social media use so that you don't miss out on the real world.

"I CAN FAST-FORWARD THE BAD PARTS"

Deciding what media to allow your tween to view may feel like a constant pressure, particularly when they start asking to watch movies and TV shows containing more adult content. It can prove more difficult if their peers are allowed to watch content with a higher age rating.

SCENARIO | You tell your tween they are too young to watch a PG-13-rated movie, and they reply that they can fast-forward through the bad parts.

Movies and TV shows stream into our homes in so many ways now, via phones and tablets as well as on TV. So tweens tend to be exposed to far more entertainment, much of it not meant for their age and some of which may include sex scenes. Sex is still a difficult and intimidating concept for tweens to get their heads around. However, modern technology enables them to stop and fast-forward through movies on streaming services, giving them more control than they have over images that pop up on the internet. This may lead them to tell you they can control how much of the movie they will view.

WHAT YOU MIGHT BE THINKING

You may feel nostalgic for the days when they wanted to watch only children's shows. You may worry what message it sends to your child if you allow them to view a movie with a higher age rating and what other parents will think if they hear about it.

" " TELL THEM AGE RATINGS HAVE BEEN DECIDED WITH CARE BY A PANEL OF EXPERTS.

WHAT THEY MIGHT BE THINKING

⊙ **Your child may be desperate not to feel left out** if some of their friends have seen the movie and have been talking about it.

⊙ **Your tween won't want you to know what they really think** about sex and will pretend they are not interested in the sex scenes, even if they are.

⊙ **Watching sex feels "awkward" to tweens** as they are watching something that is a grown-up activity, which embarrasses them.

⊙ **Despite telling you that they won't watch sex scenes,** older tweens may still watch them out of curiosity. They may lie that they fast-forwarded because they sense you are uncomfortable about their interest in finding out about sex.

HOW YOU COULD RESPOND

In the moment

Thank your tween
Tell them how pleased you are that they are asking for your guidance on what's appropriate, so they are more likely to keep you informed in the future.

Talk about age ratings
As a rule, tell them it's always better to pay attention to age ratings as these have been decided with care by a panel of experts to ensure nothing scares or confuses children before they are ready. Invite them to look at reviews with you by trusted websites like Common Sense Media, which give guidance on content and age suitability of popular movies and TV shows.

Give them control
If you watch together, let them have the remote control so they can skip over scenes that are uncomfortable for them.

In the long term

Educate them
If you decide to allow your tween to view the movie, bear in mind that sex shown in movies as part of a loving, caring relationship can be an antidote to some of the brutal, no-relationship sex shown in pornography. If there is an intimate scene in a movie you view with your tween, use it as an opportunity to talk about issues like consent and what a healthy relationship should look like.

Have movie nights
Consider having a weekly family movie night, and watch age-appropriate movies that you talk about afterward. This will send the message that your child doesn't have to watch more adult content to enjoy seeing movies.

Address violence
Violent scenes, showing deliberate cruelty, torture, bullying, coercion, and rape, can be disturbing for tweens and need to be put in adult context. Talk about the way violence becomes normalized when it is used for entertainment, and that that isn't a good thing. Explain that violence is always devastating for people when it happens in the real world.

◀ SEE RELATED TOPICS ▶
My friend showed me this video on their phone:
pp.158–159
It's online so it must be true: pp.188–189

"I AM **SO** GOING TO MARRY THEM"

An increase in sex hormones means your tween may start to feel strongly attracted to others, even if their feelings are not reciprocated. Don't dismiss these fixations as "silly" crushes; they can be a safe outlet for your child to manage romantic feelings.

SCENARIO | You spot that your tween has written their first name with the surname of their crush on their schoolbook, surrounded by love hearts.

Your tween is looking to project feelings of love. As they are not mature enough for a two-way commitment, crushes are a way of imagining what it would be like to be in a relationship. There are three categories: attraction to peers, to authority figures (teachers), and to those they don't know (celebrities). If they are fixated on a pop star, this will help define their identity, help figure out who they are attracted to, and bond them with other tweens. View crushes as an opportunity for your child to role-play in safety.

WHAT YOU MIGHT BE THINKING

You may see your tween's crush as a silly phase that will pass and worry that they are daydreaming about a relationship that will never happen.

WHAT THEY MIGHT BE THINKING

⊙ **Your tween probably doesn't know their crush well**, if at all, and will be drawn to one or two facets of their appearance or personality. This allows them to project an idealized version of the perfect partner onto them.

⊙ **As girls start puberty first**, they are likely to have crushes before boys of the same age, who may be unaware they are the objects.

Girls tend to talk about their crush more, mostly with friends and sometimes with a parent.

⊙ **Your tween may spend time daydreaming** and talking about their crush. They may imagine what it would be like to be noticed by them or seen as attractive. They may believe they are "in love" and experience the euphoria that goes with that.

◄ **SEE RELATED TOPICS** ►

How exactly are babies made?: pp.52–53
I'm doing a glow-up challenge: pp.196–197

EXPLAIN IT'S NEVER POSSIBLE TO CONTROL HOW OTHERS FEEL ABOUT THEM.

HOW YOU COULD RESPOND

In the moment

Acknowledge their feelings
Remember their feelings are real. If they keep mentioning a name, ask if they have "special feelings" for that person without embarrassing them. Ask what they admire about them and how well they know the person, to help them process their feelings and get a realistic perspective.

Be clear about boundaries
Tweens may stare at their crushes in class, or send them anonymous notes. Point out that admiration should never make someone feel uncomfortable. Explain it's never possible to control how others feel about them. Talk about how their "crush" is not an object to be admired but a complex person with thoughts, feelings, and flaws.

Put it in context
Tell them it's fine to imagine a relationship. They don't have to act on it, make it obvious, or tell anyone else about it.

In the long term

Don't make assumptions
Avoid assuming your tween's crushes are for someone of another gender. If you assume that, they may believe you approve of only one kind of relationship.

Don't focus on looks
If they have a crush on a classmate, avoid asking questions only about appearance, such as, "are they cute?" and "what do they look like?" If you do, your tween will get the message that a person's worth is based on their looks. Try other questions like: "what do you admire about them?" or "what makes them stand out?"

Talk about healthy relationships
Now that you know your tween has romantic feelings, look for opportunities to share your values about what a mature, healthy, balanced relationship should look like and how in real relationships, feelings are reciprocated equally.

BODY IMAGE

In the tween years, children can shift from thinking of their bodies as something functional that allows them to run and play and experience the world to an object that gets looked at and judged by others.

In this critical window, your tween is building their body image from many sources, including the media, as well as getting unhelpful messages from wider culture about how they "should" look. It's essential not only to stand up to these messages yourself so you don't pass them on but also to step in and help your tween learn to question them. Body anxiety, worry, and shame can interrupt a child's healthy development and, although it's impossible to prevent some of these attitudes from reaching them, it is possible to create a home where body acceptance is normal.

1
Focus on what bodies do
When children are proud of what their bodies can do, such as running, jumping, and climbing, it has a protective effect against body discomfort. Make it a family value that what's inside matters most.

4
Encourage full expression
How your child eats can become a way to express anger, rebellion, or push down shameful feelings. Always let them speak openly, even when their feelings are hard to hear.

6
Question negative self-talk
Ask them to notice thoughts like "I look fat." Suggest they see it as internal bullying. Teach them to counterbalance negative cultural messages about body shape with a mantra, such as "'My body can do amazing things."

WORKING THINGS OUT

8 key principles

2
Talk about body types
Self-acceptance is a key part of developing a positive body image. Talk about how different body types are in our genes. Explain that a healthy weight range is different for every person, based on build, height, and genetics.

3
Process your worries
Many parents were brought up at a time when judgmental attitudes about how bodies "should" look were not questioned as they are today. Be aware of any body biases you hold. Create a home in which all bodies are acceptable and where you don't criticize your own body or anyone else's.

5
Challenge ideas
If your child has taken in ideas about how the human body should look, suggest that they ask, "Who says?" Explain that there are no laws about the "ideal" body and different cultures and generations are constantly changing their views, even though human bodies are biological realities, not fashion templates. Ask them to notice, question, and talk back to any messages that make them feel like they're not good enough.

7
Take a whole family approach
If, after consulting with your doctor, there is genuine concern about your child's BMI (Body Mass Index), avoid singling out your tween. Find activities you can all do as a family, with the target of spending time together and improving well-being rather than losing weight.

8
Draw a distinction
Make it clear that meeting socially constructed ideas about appearance does not make someone more worthwhile. Avoid making moral judgments based on people's weight in front of your child.

! TAILORED ADVICE

8–10 YEARS OLD

Reassure them
Remind them that puberty changes body shape and is a natural part of growing up.

Observe other attributes
While it's fine to compliment how your child looks, put more emphasis on noticing character, behavior, and effort.

Notice the good
Once a week, have a fun ritual where you both name three things you love about your bodies and what they can do.

10–12 YEARS OLD

Build awareness
Suggest they notice hunger cues. Now that tweens can buy their own foods on the way home from school, help them observe their bodies' "full-up" signals.

Educate them
If your child is on social media, tell them it's the job of celebrities to look a certain way. Shots and clips will have been filtered, edited, or touched up.

Watch out for weight loss
It's more of a red flag for your tween to lose weight than gain it. Look for signs of your child eating in secret or big changes in eating patterns.

"I'LL CALL YOU DUDE, NOT DAD"

As a young child, your tween put you on a pedestal, viewing you as a superhero who knew everything. Now that they are seeing you more as a real person with human flaws, they may seek to redefine your relationship by changing what they call you.

SCENARIO | When you ask your tween to help you wash the car as usual, he replies: "I'll do it later, Dude," instead of "Dad."

Your child has grown up relying on you to meet their every need. For most of their childhood, you were the all-powerful center of their world who kept them safe. From around the age of nine, tweens imagine a world in which they must be independent from you. This means gaining some distance. Though they may still want to spend time with you, one way to try out this more grown-up identity is to change what they call you. This may mean switching from Mommy to Mom, Daddy to Dad—or even "Dude"—to show they are getting older and seeking autonomy.

WHAT YOU MIGHT BE THINKING

You may miss the memory of the little child who always looked up to you. By calling you something different, you may wonder if your tween is going to start resisting your authority.

WHAT THEY MIGHT BE THINKING

● **Calling you "Dude" is a clear statement** that they are no longer little and would like to be seen on a more equal footing.

● **Boys tend to show their affection for one another** by using words such as "bro," so using the word "dude" is also likely to be a sign of affection.

● **As your tween is performing for the imaginary audience** of peers in their mind, they are also trying to sound cool, hard, grown-up, and make it sound like they no longer do what you say.

● **This switch may coincide with your tween seeking out** your imperfections—and looking for flaws and inconsistencies—to make breaking away easier.

" "

SEE THIS AS YOUR TWEEN FINDING A NEW WAY TO CONNECT TO YOU.

HOW YOU COULD RESPOND

In the moment

Let it go
As long as it's meant in an affectionate rather than disrespectful way, let it pass. If you raise it, do so in a humorous, curious way and respond in kind to acknowledge the shift. You could say something like: "Wow, I've never been called Dude before. Is that what you're going to call me from now on, Bro?"

Reciprocate
Repay the compliment by asking what they'd like you to call them to mark the fact that they are older now. Ask if they now feel embarrassed by their childhood nickname, if they had one.

View it as necessary
This shift is an important part of relationship development. See it as your tween finding a new way to connect to you and a move toward developing their identity as an independent person. However, make it clear that they are still expected to be respectful.

In the long term

Moms, be prepared
As boys start turning into men, they look to male parents and other male role models to figure out how to act and be. So this inevitably involves moving a little away from you and trying to relate to Dads on more of a friend level.

Look for other outlets
Find ways for your tween to bond with you on a more mature footing, whether it's getting involved in a grown-up creative project together or working toward a more adult fitness goal.

Let them feel equal
Be encouraging and supportive of your tween as they experiment with being mature, rather than being preoccupied with maintaining the same unquestioned authority you had over your child when they were younger. See your tween calling you "Dude" as a sign that they are secure enough in their relationship with you to move the boundaries.

SEE RELATED TOPICS
I hate you!: pp.94–95
Don't tell me what to do!: pp.118–119

"I'M GETTING **SPOTS**"

As your child's hormones change, the appearance of spots from skin acne may take you both by surprise. Depending on how much the spots bother your tween, you may need to offer emotional and practical support.

SCENARIO | Your child looks in the bathroom mirror in the morning and notices they have spots on their face. They tell you they are concerned.

Over the course of adolescence, around 9 out of 10 young people will have spots. The age of the onset of puberty is happening earlier across the world, possibly due to changes in nutrition and chemicals in the environment. It's as young as eight for girls and nine for boys. As acne linked to puberty lasts between five and ten years on average, it will help to get your tween into good skincare habits from an early age. While your tween may not yet be bothered, acne is now recognized as a skin disease, so keep a subtle eye out for it getting worse and affecting their confidence.

WHAT YOU MIGHT BE THINKING

If you are used to your tween having childlike skin, you may be nostalgic for the time when it needed no attention. You may also worry your tween will feel self-conscious among their peers.

SEE RELATED TOPICS
I don't want a bath tonight: pp.30–31
I am not pretty enough: pp.104–105

WHAT THEY MIGHT BE THINKING

⊙ **A skincare regime is new:** until now, all your tween had to do to look after their body was bathe, brush their teeth, and brush their hair. So it may take time to get used to looking after their complexion too.

⊙ **Your tween may be confused** as to why they are seeing black dots—or blackheads—on their nose, or why a bump can appear randomly anywhere on their face.

⊙ **Your tween may not be bothered** by their skin if they don't yet think a lot about their appearance or whether they are attractive. If they are bothered by their spots, they might be frustrated that washing their face won't make the spots go away.

⊙ **Your tween may be tempted to squeeze spots** then not know how to cover them up if that makes them worse.

HOW YOU COULD RESPOND

In the moment

Avoid making a fuss
If the changes in their skin don't bother your tween, don't let them bother you either, or you will send the message that their worth is linked to how they look.

Listen to them
If they are concerned, say something like: "It sounds as if your skin is bothering you. It's not your fault that you have developed acne. If you'd like to, we can figure out some ways to look after your skin." Make it clear that acne is a disease that starts deep within the skin, so it's not caused by anything they have done, though they can take steps that should help.

Work with them on a routine
Take your tween to the store to find some gentle skincare products, to help them take ownership. Spend time showing them how to get into a regular routine of washing their face every time they brush their teeth.

In the long term

Give alternatives to squeezing spots
A spot will feel like a foreign body that your tween wants to eliminate. Squeezing them can be unhealthy and a coping mechanism for worry. If you notice this, suggest that your tween identifies triggers and talks to you. Suggest applying a face mask or pressing an ice cube on a spot. Some people use brightly colored acne patches as fashion statements. Congratulate them for leaving spots alone.

Give context
If your tween is among the first to get spots in their class, explain that almost all of their peers will get spots eventually and will be more likely to sympathize.

Be positive
There is a growing movement to challenge the notion of "good" and "bad" skin and take the stigma out of acne.

ANXIETY

Worry is our brain's natural way of preparing for challenges that haven't happened yet. But if worrying starts to interfere with your child's life and stops them from going to school, being apart from you, or trying new things, they may develop anxiety.

Anxiety is when a tween overestimates a threat and believes they will be unable to cope. To parents, it can show up as developing phobias, being irritable or fidgety, not eating and sleeping properly, negative thinking, being overly self-conscious, being clingy, having trouble sleeping, or experiencing stomach pain and headaches. Temperament, genetics, and triggers at school can all play their part. But caring, thoughtful adults can help young people calm their fears and manage these feelings. For high-achieving tweens, perfectionist tendencies can develop during this period, due to the validation they get from school and parents when they do well. This can develop into anxiety as they get older. Check that you are not encouraging this, consciously or unconsciously, and give tweens permission to scrap unrealistic targets so they don't fear failure.

" "

HELP YOUR TWEEN RATIONALIZE HOW REAL A THREAT IS AND SOOTHE THEMSELF WITH COPING TALK.

1

Make them self-aware
Help children learn to spot the signs they are getting overwhelmed. Suggest a visual, such as a set of traffic lights, to help tweens notice and say how they feel: green means they are in the present and able to think clearly; yellow indicates they are getting a little anxious; red is a sign that their thoughts and body are getting affected by anxiety.

4

Teach breathing
Show your tween how to manage their nervous system response. Try balloon breathing. Ask them to imagine a balloon in their tummy, then slowly breathe in for a count of three, and slowly exhale. They can fill the balloon with thoughts of stress and tension until they are ready to release it focusing on the exhale.

WORKING THINGS OUT

6 key principles

2

Reduce cortisol levels

Research is finding that children are flooded with more of the stress hormone cortisol than in the past. When those levels stay high, this dampens the effect of well-being neurochemicals, such as serotonin and oxytocin, that give children the sense all is well. Make your home feel like a safe place, avoid adding academic pressure, and make space for play, nature activities, and regular family time, allowing everyone's cortisol levels to reset.

3

Explain what is happening

Anxiety is triggered when our brains overestimate the level of a threat. The early warning system, the amygdala, goes into high alert and sends messages to increase stress hormones in the body. The amygdala reacts whether we're being chased by a lion or anticipating a math test. Help your tween tell the difference so that they can assess how real a threat is and soothe themselves with coping talk, such as: "I'll get through this."

5

Limit screen use

Children's anxiety has risen with the amount they are exposed to the news: crime, war, political instability, disease, climate change, or fake news. They may be seeing nuggets of the most extreme events repeated on social media like TikTok. Limit consumption of news to child-safe sources, which give context, and, if possible, look at this news alongside them so you can discuss it afterward.

6

Manage your anxiety

Animal and human studies have both found that when parents are stressed, their offspring are stressed too. This is because young animals look for cues from adults to show them how to be in the world. If you are feeling stressed, process your worries with the help of another caring adult.

TAILORED ADVICE

8–10
YEARS OLD

Help them be expressive
Find ways for your child to express their worries. Don't dismiss or shame them. Ask questions and role-play with toys or ask them to draw what's bothering them.

Use brave talk
Point out the worries they have overcome in the past, so they feel empowered.

Find coping strategies
Whether it's a cuddle with a pet or baking, encourage your child to find a toolbox of ways to feel better.

10–12
YEARS OLDS

Channel eco-anxiety
As environmental worries rise at this age, encourage your tween to channel their feelings into making a difference.

Keep regular bedtimes
Not getting enough sleep over time increases the risk of anxiety in children, as they find it harder to manage overwhelming feelings when tired and can feel more irritable.

Say it's normal
Tweens often think there's something wrong if they are stressed. Explain that worry is a normal part of being human and it motivates us to act.

"I'M SCARED I WON'T GET A GOOD GRADE"

Children are educated in a system where success is measured by a narrowing set of academic standards. As they move into senior school, your tween may start measuring their personal worth by the test grades they achieve.

SCENARIO | Your tween tells you they struggled in their end-of-year science exam and are worried they'll get a bad result.

If your tween tends to find academic work easy and has been told they should aim high, they may increasingly thrive on the approval they get for good grades. However, this can create a drive for perfectionism, which can run high particularly in girls who are more likely to want to be seen as "good" and rate their worth by their results. As they are prone to black-and-white thinking, and don't yet have the perspective to know there are many ways to succeed, your tween may panic that they won't be able to live up to these internalized expectations. This may lead them to catastrophize about what will happen if they fall short.

WHAT YOU MIGHT BE THINKING

You may be eager for your tween to do well but be worried that they are putting so much pressure on themself to excel that they won't be able to cope.

WHAT THEY MIGHT BE THINKING

◉ **Instead of congratulating themself**, being a perfectionist may lead your tween to focus on grades they don't get on the test rather than the ones they do.

◉ **Your tween may find that working harder** is the only way to ease their worry, but this can cause them to only want to submit "perfect" work—or feel they must get the top grades on every test.

◉ **If your tween is friends with a high-achieving group** of peers, they will feel under even more social pressure to keep up as they will be comparing results.

◉ **Your child may feel proud of getting their target grade** but believe they have to sacrifice downtime for studying. They may worry about how to maintain high grades.

> **MAKE IT CLEAR THAT YOUR CHILD IS MORE THAN THE SUM OF THEIR ACHIEVEMENTS.**

HOW YOU COULD RESPOND

In the moment

Thank them
It is important to praise your tween for telling you, and to listen. Perfectionist children can stop expressing their needs for fear of letting others down.

Don't criticize
Avoid saying they put too much pressure on themself as this will make it sound like it's their fault. They are likely to feel this anyway due to factors ranging from family expectations to cultural messages about what success is.

Pull back
If you have asked about revision a lot, your tween may get the message that their grade is the only thing that matters.

Encourage self-compassion
If a lot of "musts" and "shoulds" are running through their mind, suggest they replace them with more compassionate words like "try," "attempt," and "perhaps." Help them access more helpful thoughts by imagining what a kind best friend would say.

In the long term

Praise other qualities
Make it clear that your child is more than the sum of their achievements. Celebrate their qualities, like humor or empathy. Remind your tween that exams don't give grades for character, persistence, and creativity.

Watch your words
You may say you just want your child to be happy, but are they hearing: "We want you to be happy as long as you don't disappoint us"? Are you pegging your hopes on a good exam result because it will reflect well on you? Unpick these feelings as your tween is likely to pick up on them.

Encourage self-satisfaction
"Extrinsic" motivation is when we want to do well for others, and "intrinsic" is when we get satisfaction from doing something for us, and is linked to higher achievement long-term. Support your tween in wanting to make progress for themself, not for others. Ask them how it feels.

SEE RELATED TOPICS
I am doing my homework: pp.66–67
I don't want to go to school: pp.108–109

"MY SELFIE GOT **100 LIKES!**"

Your tween may use a camera phone to experiment with different ways to present themself. If they post images to social media, it can set up a feedback loop in which they depend on getting "likes" to feel good.

SCENARIO | Your tween is thrilled to get so many positive reactions to the selfies they post while on vacation.

Tweens can take selfies for many reasons. They can be a way of sending peers virtual "waves." As tweens start to compare themselves to their peers and celebrities, they may begin to experiment with their image. This is part of the development of the "looking-glass self"—a phase in which adolescents start to become more preoccupied with how others see them, and it can impact their view of themselves. When tweens post selfies, they are taking control of the image they present to others and are trying to find out if they are attractive. If they don't get the response they want, they may try to construct "an ideal self" with the help of filtering apps and then post selfies that are hard to live up to in real life.

WHAT YOU MIGHT BE THINKING

You may be annoyed your tween is taking so many pictures of themselves, thinking they are being "silly," are becoming "self-obsessed," and are inviting negative comments.

◆ **SEE RELATED TOPICS** ◆
I'm going to be famous when I grow up:
pp.110–111
I'm doing a glow-up challenge: pp.196–197

WHAT THEY MIGHT BE THINKING

⊚ **Your tween is happy with 100 likes** because it makes them feel in control of their image, popular, powerful, and attractive.

⊚ **They compare themself to peers.** Your tween may take 20 selfies, agonize over which to post, then remove it if it does not get as many likes as their peers.

⊚ **They want to experiment with their looks** so might be imitating sexualized poses of celebrities without understanding how they might be perceived. In your tween's mind, getting attention for their looks equals popularity.

⊚ **"Likes" give your tween a dopamine hit.** But when they don't get the approval they are seeking, levels of the status neurotransmitters serotonin and dopamine will fall, and levels of the stress hormone cortisol will rise. They may keep posting selfies to try to feel good again.

" "

SUGGEST THAT YOUR TWEEN TRACKS WHETHER THEY POST MORE WHEN THEY FEEL INSECURE.

HOW YOU COULD RESPOND

In the moment

Explore why they are posting
If they are not trying to get sexual attention, or posing for the judgment of others, there's no need to worry.

Change the focus
Help your tween with ideas about how they could use their camera to capture the wonders of the world instead.

Encourage privacy
Ask if they need to post selfies. Could they keep them as memories instead, or send them to a group of friends or family, rather than invite comments from strangers?

Empower them
Studies show that girls post more selfies when feeling less powerful. Help your tween feel more in control through activities such as sports, music, art, or movement. Remind them they have strong bodies, minds, and imaginations that make them capable.

In the long term

Curate the social media feed
Talk about steering their feed toward social causes or interests other than appearance. Tell them to set their account to private to avoid uninvited comments.

Get them thinking
Suggest they think about how the image may be viewed. Do they want to be judged? How will a spiteful remark make them feel? Does the photo show "the real them"? Is counting the number of likes stressful and distracting?

Suggest boundaries
Studies show the more time tweens spend on social media, the worse they feel about their appearance. Encourage them to look out for signs that it is triggering anxiety. Research also shows the more tweens judge their bodies, the more selfies they take. Suggest that your tween tracks whether they post more when they feel insecure—this will help them recognize external pressure.

"I'M SO BAD AT SPORTS"

As tweens get stronger, faster, and more coordinated, as well as bond through shared activities, being skillful at sports becomes more important to them, both at school and in their social lives.

SCENARIO | Your tween tells you they are "useless" because no one wanted them on their soccer team at break time.

For evolutionary reasons, sporting skill is highly prized and respected among groups of tweens. Boys can feel under particular cultural pressure to be seen as good at sports. Because athletic power is often seen as a form of masculine authority, athletic boys tend to get placed higher up the social hierarchy. Girls can also feel marginalized and belittled by more athletic classmates if they are viewed as "bad" at sports.

WHAT YOU MIGHT BE THINKING

You may worry about how such disappointments will affect your child's self-esteem. It may feel like unfair treatment, making you feel angry toward the children who are leaving your tween out.

REMIND THEM THEY DON'T HAVE TO BE THE BEST TO BE A VALUED TEAM MEMBER.

WHAT THEY MIGHT BE THINKING

⊚ **Winning and losing is now more serious** among your tween and their friends. Their sporting ability is becoming more obvious as they play competitively.

⊚ **Your son may receive a cultural message** that he is failing if he's not sporty, as competitiveness and strength are traditionally seen as masculine traits.

⊚ **Tweens will be annoyed if others dismiss them** for not liking sports. Your tween will feel hurt when more skillful players are picked for teams and could be stuck for what else to do at break times.

⊚ **Your tween may distance themself**, pretending not to care, or claiming those good at sports are "stupid." They may seek to strengthen other skills, so they stand out for other reasons.

HOW YOU COULD RESPOND

In the moment

Listen
Rather than jump in to deny your child's feelings and try to make yourself feel better, let your tween explain why they feel the way they do. Acknowledge rather than dismiss how they feel.

Hone in on the details
Tweens are prone to all-or-nothing catastrophic thinking. Ask them what they mean by "bad at sports"? Do they just feel this today or all the time? Have they played well at other times or been picked at other times?

In the long term

Find a different voice
Explain that having a negative inner voice will make them more stressed and less likely to play well. Suggest that they replace this inner critic with the voice of an encouraging coach.

Offer alternatives
At a neutral time, suggest to your child that they may have to try a range of activities before they find the one they love. This could range from martial arts to dance or swimming. The point is to keep fit and have fun.

Find a break-time club
Suggest they join a club that focuses on another activity, so they meet peers with similar interests. Having others who like the same activities will reassure them their interests are okay too.

Discuss growth mindset
When your child is not upset, mention that we all develop skills at different speeds. If they want to improve at sports, practice at home. Remind them they don't have to be the best to be a valued team member. Most people's abilities lie in the middle.

Encourage both genders
When girls value their bodies for what they can do, such as play sports, rather than how they look, it can protect against body image worries in the future.

Deal with your own feelings
Whether you imagined watching your child scoring goals galore or were determined they would never be picked last for the team as you were, let go of the past. Meet your child where they are.

◀ SEE RELATED TOPICS ▶
I'm a loser: pp.92–93
I want to give up: pp.122–123

PORNOGRAPHY

Many parents prefer not to think about tweens even seeing pornography on the internet, but unfortunately, we live in an age where it's not a question of if our children will see it but when.

By the age of nine, 1 in 10 children have seen pornography. By the age of 11, a quarter of children have been exposed to it, and the figure continues to climb as kids enter their teenage years. Initially, most children don't go looking for porn; they come across it when they click on the wrong websites or misspell web addresses. Or it finds them via links or hidden among social media videos. Your tween may also be shown porn by other children on smartphones. Later, as puberty kicks in, and they become curious about sex, the obvious place to look is the internet, where the lack of age restrictions mean they will find thousands of hard-core, and often violent clips, within seconds.

1
Address the issue early
Research shows that most parents don't raise the subject until after a child has seen porn. Bringing up the subject with children in age-appropriate ways as they grow up helps to prepare them and can minimize potential harm.

4
Keep it simple
Explain that there is content online that is not for children, showing violence and cruelty. Make it clear your tween will not get into trouble for showing you images that frighten or confuse them.

6
Keep talking
Make it clear you are always available to talk. View it as a health issue—as important as talking about drugs or alcohol—because it can also trigger addictive behaviors.

WORKING THINGS OUT

8 key principles

2

Prepare them for it
As they get older, tell them the more time they spend online, the more likely it is they will come across pornography and it's likely to be confusing. Reassure them what they will see does not represent real sex or body parts, in the same way that an action movie isn't true to real life.

3

Talk about making love first
First talk about intimacy and how ideally, sex is a special, tender activity that grown-ups do in private, along with hugging and kissing, that helps them feel closer to one another.

> " "
>
> ## TELL THEM WHAT THEY SEE DOES NOT REPRESENT REAL SEX, JUST AS AN ACTION MOVIE ISN'T TRUE TO LIFE.

5

Don't assume it's just boys
Viewing porn is more frequent and deliberate among boys, but girls view it too. Even if they don't return to it, it can create harmful expectations about how they should behave and be treated.

7

Talk about future relationships
As your tween starts to form romantic feelings, talk about how the happiest, most fulfilling sex involves affection and activities that both parties feel comfortable with. Explain that porn is created to make money and to shock.

8

Educate them
As tweens get older, explain that studies show watching porn can activate the same reward centers in the brain as recreational drugs and make it harder to become aroused in real relationships.

TAILORED ADVICE

8–10
YEARS OLD

Tell them what to do
Make it clear to your tween that if they see porn, they are not in trouble. Tell them they should exit the screen immediately and then tell a grown-up.

Close down access
Look for app and website tools that can help delay first exposure for as long as possible.

10–12
YEARS OLD

Ask them not to share
Research shows that older tweens are more likely to forward on sexually explicit videos to friends because they want to see how others react. Point out the shock and distress it can cause to others.

Be indirect
As they get older, your tween may clam up if you try to talk directly about porn. To try to prevent this, approach the subject indirectly. Try saying something like: "I read that a lot of boys have seen porn by the age of 11. That seems young. What do you think?"

"MY TEACHER **HATES ME!**"

Teachers give children their first experiences of dealing with adult authority figures outside of their families. So if your child feels a teacher doesn't like them, they may feel hurt and powerless to change their opinion.

SCENARIO | When you ask your tween how school was, they complain they had a bad day because their teacher "hates" them.

As they form their identities, tweens find themselves in a constant process of asking, "Am I likable?" As teachers have a huge influence over their lives, being liked by them will be important. They are not yet at the stage when they will question authority, so they assume teachers are all-powerful, all-knowing beings. If they feel unliked by them, they will assume it's their own fault. They will also feel vulnerable and angry if they feel picked on by a teacher in the public theater of the classroom, in front of their peers.

WHAT YOU MIGHT BE THINKING

You may feel protective because it may bring back memories of feeling disliked by a teacher from your own school days.

WHAT THEY MIGHT BE THINKING

⊙ **A teacher's opinion matters a lot to your tween.** As children this age are black-and-white thinkers, they may think one correction means their teacher will never like them.

⊙ **As a way to vent pent-up feelings**, your tween may say they hate their teacher after a tiring day at school, when they had to stick to rules set by powerful adults all day.

⊙ **They may use the excuse that their teacher is picking on them** to deflect responsibility for their actions if your tween has been corrected for misbehaving or not paying attention.

⊙ **Your tween will have developed a sensitive antenna** for fairness. If they feel other pupils are more favored, they may think this is hypocritical and will feel justified in being angry.

◆ **SEE RELATED TOPICS** ▶
I don't want to go to school: pp.108–109
I'm scared I won't get a good grade:
pp.138–139

HOW YOU COULD RESPOND

In the moment

Listen
Once your tween has offloaded the frustrations of their day, they may feel better. Listening to their complaints, without trying to give advice or "fix" the uncomfortable feelings, will help your child process them.

Be curious
If they want to talk, ask open, nonjudgmental questions about what leads them to believe this. Tweens can be egocentric, so ask them to imagine how their behavior might look from the teacher's point of view.

Don't agree too readily
While being available to soothe your child, bear in mind that tweens are prone to all-or-nothing thinking and overgeneralizing. While you may feel protective, jumping to agree with their view that their teacher hates them could feed your tween's view of themselves as a victim.

In the long term

Depersonalize it
At some point, your child will learn they will not be liked by everyone, including people with power over them, such as educators and bosses. Praise them for their "professionalism" when they do their best in their lessons anyway.

Suggest a growth mindset
Explain that teachers don't only favor students who excel but also those who listen and make an effort. Suggest that your tween is more likely to be met with a positive response from a teacher if they are polite and willing to do the tasks. Reassure them that even if things don't improve with this particular teacher, it won't be long before they have a new teacher with whom they can have a different relationship.

Be tactful
If the problem persists, the next time you have a parent-teacher meeting, start with the assumption that the teacher is trying their best with your child and that you don't have the whole story. Using "I feel" statements, say something like: "I'm sure you mean to improve my child's motivation, but in my child's case, they seem to feel demoralized." Be ready to hear the teacher's perspective. This feedback may help the teacher understand your child's feelings and take steps to reset their relationship.

"WHEN WILL I GET MY PERIOD?"

As your daughter's puberty progresses, she may start to worry more about when she will get her first period and whether it will take her by surprise. She will need your help to prepare for this important milestone.

SCENARIO | Your daughter heard that a friend got her first period while she was in a class and asks how she can make sure that won't happen to her.

While the average age of girls getting their first period has dropped to around 12 years, they can start as early as age 8 or as late as age 16. There will be some signs in the run-up, such as developing breasts, pubic hair, and an increase in vaginal discharge, but it's never possible to pinpoint the arrival of a first period. The uncertainty can lay heavily on girls. However, parental reassurance and preparation goes a long way toward helping their first period be a positive experience.

WHAT YOU MIGHT BE THINKING

You may feel helpless to know what to tell your daughter, as it's never possible to tell when a first period will arrive. It may bring back memories of your own worries about when yours would start.

WHAT THEY MIGHT BE THINKING

⊚ **Your tween thinks logically based on her experiences**. So if the only time she has seen blood is when she has cut or injured herself, she may be scared.

⊚ **Her head may be filled with fear of what will happen** if classmates spot signs, like leaks on her clothes at school, due to sensitivity to her peers, and the "imaginary audience" in her head.

⊚ **Your tween may be hearing gossip** about who has and hasn't started their periods in their class. She may hope that her period comes soon so she can join these conversations.

⊚ **She may see starting her period as the sign of becoming** "a woman" and feel less mature and experienced than other girls until hers starts too.

SEE RELATED TOPICS
I need a bra: pp.102–103
They tease me about my boobs: pp.152–153

HOW YOU COULD RESPOND

In the moment

Talk about timings
Explain timings are different for everyone, and the start of her first period can't be sped up or slowed down. But while there's no way she can ever be certain when it will arrive, she can be prepared, and after that, her periods are likely to be more regular.

Put together a period pack
Together, create a pack of sanitary pads, clean underwear, and disposal bags in a pencil case to keep in her school bag. Help her feel prepared by showing how to stick pads onto underwear securely. Show her how to dispose of used pads, reminding her never to flush them down a toilet.

Prepare her for accidents
Make her feel empowered by showing how she can cope, whatever happens. Talk about how she could improvise by making a wad of toilet paper until she gets a pad from a friend or grown-up. Show her how to tie a sweater or sweatshirt around her waist to conceal leaks.

Put it in perspective
Explain the amount of blood that will come out is between four and six tablespoons, and it comes out over between four and eight days.

Help her spot the signs
It's impossible to pinpoint the date of a first period, but she will spot clues in the lead-up. Often a period appears about two years after breasts start to grow, and she will notice a milky vaginal discharge in the year to six months before.

In the long term

Ask what questions she has
Tweens will fill in the gaps with things they've heard from classmates or social media. Asking your daughter what she's heard will allow you to clear up any confusion and help her feel more in control.

Be positive
Emphasize the female body is amazing and that, with a bit of experience, periods shouldn't interfere with anything she wants to do, including swimming and sports, thanks to period swimwear and tampons. When her period arrives, ask her if she'd like to do something special together to mark it. Then help her see managing her period as an important part of self-care.

> **MAKE HER FEEL EMPOWERED BY SHOWING HOW SHE CAN COPE, WHATEVER HAPPENS.**

STEPFAMILIES

If you have created a stepfamily, it is important to prioritize your tween's needs and work to create a new household where they feel safe and welcome.

Tweens are at a vulnerable stage of development where adults' opinions are important to their self-worth. They may also have enough experience and memories of their original family to mourn and be angry about the loss. As they are in an egotistical phase of thinking, they may feel insecure and believe that one or both parents did not love them enough to stay together for them. If there is shared custody, they may feel awkward, homesick, or in the way in a parent's new home. To cope, their reactions may vary. As a defense mechanism, they may appear withdrawn and aggressive—particularly toward a stepparent whom they do not like—or they may go to the other extreme to become overly people-pleasing and compliant in the hope of being loved and accepted into the new family unit.

1
Be a team
Have a good relationship with your stepchild's other natural parent. Remove the emotion and make it a shared goal to put the health and happiness of your stepchild first.

4
Set aside one-to-one time
If you're the stepparent, build a relationship with your stepchild by making time to connect—find activities you like to do together, avoiding overlap with the other natural parent's territory.

7
Let them grieve
If there's a wedding or baby on the way, this could end hopes of parents reuniting, triggering tween's fears they will be forgotten. Invite them to get involved in planning so they feel included.

WORKING THINGS OUT

8 key principles

2

Stay patient

It can take many years for stepfamilies to feel like a unit. You will be able to handle the challenges more calmly if both you and your partner have reasonable expectations of how long it will take. Time, effort, and empathy are required.

3

Make it clear you're on their side

Tweens may feel they have to work hard at being accepted and liked by their parent's new partner. Notice the good things they do, celebrate their successes, and involve them in family life. Assure them they can be loved by everyone.

5

Acknowledge difficult emotions

Tell your tween you appreciate how hard it must be to see their mother or father love an adult who isn't their parent, who they didn't choose. Even if it's painful to hear, manage your own feelings, and let them express themself so they feel heard.

6

Think carefully about discipline

As a stepparent, agree on rules with your partner, their former partner, and your stepchild. Play a supporting role, but let the original parents impose discipline. Nothing causes more resentment than a stepparent stepping into the role of disciplinarian without authority.

8

Tackle stepsibling rivalry head-on

It's never possible to foresee how tweens will get on with new stepsiblings. The normal resentments that erupt between siblings may be magnified. Get together at the start to draw up a general set of family rules so everyone feels treated equally and make it clear each child will be loved uniquely. Give children a forum to express their feelings, such as family meetings or a suggestions box.

TAILORED ADVICE

8–10 YEARS OLD

Show it wasn't their fault

If you are the natural parent and your tween overheard you argue with their other parent about them, they may think the split is their fault. Make it clear there were many reasons for your breakup; it had nothing to do with them.

Create continuity

Moving between homes can feel chaotic. Agree with your former partner to keep the same bedtime and mealtime routines, as well as playdates and family get-togethers. Try to give your tween their own space and possessions at both homes.

10–12 YEARS OLD

Be flexible

As your tween forges their social life, be flexible about visitation nights or weekends. Avoid seeing this as a rejection or inconvenience to family life.

Be accepting

As the contract for their family life was broken, they may feel they can behave as they like. Make it clear that you and your partner have open arms, while maintaining boundaries and expectations about behavior.

"THEY TEASE ME ABOUT **MY BOOBS**"

When it comes to puberty, tweens want to fit in, rather than stand out by developing too early or too late. If your child starts puberty sooner, they will need extra help to navigate changes that begin before they are ready to handle them.

SCENARIO | Your daughter comes home crying because in the changing rooms before PE, another girl said she should be wearing a bra.

If your tween experiences precocious puberty—before the age of eight for girls and nine for boys—or is the first to develop among their peer group, they may feel embarrassed for standing out and alone with their body changes. For girls, breast development can be challenging because it is so visible. While you can't control the development that puberty brings, there are many ways you can help your child manage it and make sure they continue to enjoy their tween years as the children they are.

WHAT YOU MIGHT BE THINKING

It may feel like your tween's childhood is coming to an end. You may struggle if people are noticing that your child's body is changing and are treating them as older than they are.

SEE RELATED TOPICS
I need a bra: pp.102–103,
When will I get my period?: pp.148–149

WHAT THEY MIGHT BE THINKING

⊚ **A girl with early breast development** may be confused and overwhelmed by the changes in her body and try to hide them by wearing layers or crossing her arms over her chest.

⊚ **Your tween may become self-conscious** about her peers spotting signs of puberty at times when they have to get changed, such as at swimming lessons. They may worry that they are being talked about by other classmates. They will also be curious about the changes they are going through.

⊚ **A girl may complain that boys** are noticing and looking at her differently and she will not know how to respond.

HOW YOU COULD RESPOND

In the moment

Address the issue
Listen to what happened and give your tween plenty of hugs, as they will want to feel like the child they are. Avoid making it sound like early puberty is a health problem. You could say: "I know your body may be growing a little quicker, but you are still the age you are."

Talk openly
When discussing with your tween, avoid referring to the changes puberty brings as something to be ashamed of. Tell them you are always available to answer questions. Although it may be startling to see your child with a more adult body sooner than expected, process your worries out of their hearing.

Look ahead
Talk to your child about how these developments are preparing them for adulthood, which is many years in the future. Remind yourself that puberty and readiness for sex are not the same thing, and at this stage there is no need for your tween to associate them. Instead of viewing puberty as the start of adulthood, see it as another stage of childhood.

Talk about body difference
Explain that everyone goes through puberty at some stage, but that it can happen at different rates. Tell your child that they have started earlier, which just means their bodies look more grown-up.

In the long term

Help regulate their emotions
Tweens experiencing puberty are not yet emotionally equipped to deal with the hormone surges that can affect mood. Remember they still have a limited ability to calm down by themselves. Employ the same approach as you did with toddler tantrums, by being a comforting presence until they can regulate their emotions again. Offer plenty of comfort and reassurance. Stick to the normal routines for a child their age, like story times.

Keep your tween active
Help your child use their body in active ways so they see strength and height as something to be proud of. Talk about how everyone's bodies are different.

Be attentive
If your child continues to develop at a faster rate, contact your family physician. Unchecked, precocious puberty can prevent your child from reaching their full adult height.

TALK ABOUT HOW THESE CHANGES ARE PREPARING THEM FOR ADULTHOOD, WHICH IS YEARS IN THE FUTURE.

"WHAT'S HAPPENING TO MY VOICE?"

One of the most obvious signs of puberty in a boy is when his voice gets deeper. However, as a boy's voice box changes and settles to its new pitch, it may waver or squeak when he talks.

SCENARIO | Your son tells you that at break time his friends teased him about his voice going up and down.

As boys go through puberty, they build more muscle mass. Testosterone bulks up the vocal cords, which are two bands of muscle. Over time, these become 60 percent longer and thicker and vibrate at a lower frequency when air passes through, making male voices sound deeper. As a boy gets bigger, his nasal, sinus, and throat cavities will also get larger, making his voice resonate more. Some boys' voices start to change as early as age 11. During this transition, a boy can lose control over his voice, and it can crack. For many boys, this passes quickly, but others, who are self-conscious, may talk less until it levels out.

WHAT YOU MIGHT BE THINKING

You may feel nostalgic that your boy seems to be growing into a man and curious about what other changes are happening that you can't see. You may fear losing some authority now that your son is getting a louder adult voice.

WHAT THEY MIGHT BE THINKING

⊙ **Your tween is likely to be embarrassed** if his voice is breaking sooner than average, because it's a public sign of private bodily changes that include an increase in penis and testicle size.

⊙ **Your tween may talk less in class, if he is teased** by classmates or family. He may spend more time alone, or stop talking as much generally.

⊙ **Your son wants to know when his voice will finally settle.** If he sings, he will worry about what his voice will be like afterward and how low it will go.

⊙ **As your tween gets older, his social group will be divided** into boys with higher, more childlike voices and deeper, more adult tones. Though the transition may be embarrassing for now, your tween will know that deep voices command more authority and power.

HOW YOU COULD RESPOND

In the moment

Thank him
Say you are pleased he has told you and tell him that you understand he must feel vulnerable and self-conscious while his voice is wavering.

Explain what happens
Tell your tween: "As you breathe out through your windpipe, air passes through your voice box. Now that your vocal cords are getting denser and stronger, like a thicker guitar string, the sound they make is deeper." Compare it to tuning up an instrument until it hits the right pitch.

Reassure him
Assure him it won't last forever. Some boys' voices change gradually, whereas others adjust more quickly. Dads can talk about how their own voice broke at around the same age, to help boys look forward to being on the other side of the change.

In the long term

Brief others
Ask relatives not to comment. If you have a daughter who is making fun of her brother, explain that girls' voices also deepen with time, only less obviously.

Keep chatting
For some boys, feeling self-conscious about their voice can mark the start of them talking less than girls do throughout adolescence. Having a deeper voice may also make them feel like they should leave "babyish" chat behind. Find opportunities to connect over a shared activity where your son will be thinking less about how he sounds, like gaming or a bike ride.

Encourage singing
Research has found that some boys who enjoy singing give up at this stage because they are worried about their voice cracking. However, continuing to practice and control their breathing can help them control their newly beefed-up vocal cords. If your son is in a choir, suggest he asks his teacher to give him a lower singing part during the transition.

SEE RELATED TOPICS
How tall will I get?: pp.170–171
I didn't mean to punch the wall: pp.176–177

"SHE'S A **SLUT**"

As tween boys become more aware of girls, they may not realize they have absorbed distorted societal and cultural messages about sexual relationships. They will need your guidance to help them think about what's influencing their choice of words.

SCENARIO | When you are driving your son and his friend to a party, you hear him jokingly call a female classmate a "slut."

Tweens increasingly become conscious of each other as future romantic partners. To save themselves from the pain of rejection, and to fit in with their male peers, boys may resort to sexist language to distance themselves from their complex feelings and to create an aura of what they think is adult "masculinity." While boys may use the word "slut," "sket," or "slag" to casually dismiss girls as worthless, girls may use it against one another. This is because they have figured out it's a powerful way to ruin the reputation of a girl they view as a rival, one who is attracting attention for being more confident or who is developing at a faster rate than they are.

WHAT YOU MIGHT BE THINKING

You may be shocked to hear your child use such an insult and wonder if they understand the meaning of this harsh sexual term. You may wonder how they know it.

WHAT THEY MIGHT BE THINKING

⊙ **Tweens will test the impact of taboo words.** They have not yet questioned the double standards of words like "slut" and will try them out to see how shocking or funny their peers find them.

⊙ **They may have heard older kids using this word,** because it is used in porn and misogynistic social media to justify demeaning acts against women. Your son may have observed how using this word makes boys sound powerful.

⊙ **If tween boys are attracted to girls who don't notice them,** calling them "sluts" is a way of making themselves feel better by saying girls are worthless anyway.

⊙ **Boys can fear being shamed by their male peers as weak,** wimpy, or unmanly and may believe that using this word asserts their masculinity. If you challenge them, they may defend name-calling as just something that boys do.

▶ **SEE RELATED TOPICS** ◀
It's not gross, it's funny!: pp.80–81,
I dare you!: pp.162–163

HOW YOU COULD RESPOND

In the moment

Intervene
Ask your son about his choice of words. By saying nothing, you will be tacitly condoning its use.

Encourage self-reflection
Ask your child to consider different perspectives. Why has he used this word? Would he say it to the girl's face? How does he think it would feel to be called this?

Talk about its effect
Once you've listened, share your adult perspective. Do not shame him, and keep it brief. Tell him how words matter—that they have power and can be hurtful. The word "slut" dehumanizes the person it's used against.

In the long term

Discuss double standards
Ask your tween why they think girls are shamed for perceived sexual activity, while boys are praised for it. Ask them to think about why there's no equivalent to commonly used insults like "slut" for boys.

Be a good role model
Your tween will be getting many societal and cultural messages about sex and gender. So push back by making equality and fairness important values in your home. Show your son that equality benefits all genders because it allows everyone to reach their potential without limits. Point out that whoever he meets in life is worthy of dignity and courtesy.

" "

MAKE EQUALITY AND FAIRNESS IMPORTANT VALUES IN YOUR HOME.

"MY FRIEND SHOWED ME **THIS** VIDEO ON THEIR PHONE"

While the internet is an unparalleled learning tool that gives teenagers instant access to a vast bank of information, it has also made it much more likely that tweens will have early exposure to sexually graphic clips that they are not developmentally ready to see.

SCENARIO | Your child is quiet and tearful after school. When you ask why, they say a classmate showed a pornographic video on their phone on the bus.

As tweens tend to have access to phones, it means they can scan the internet unsupervised and access portals to see porn. As there are no age restrictions, they can find explicit and extreme content within seconds. Even if they don't go looking for it, they may stumble across it online or be shown it by peers or older children who have gadgets of their own. As the landing page of the most popular and highest-ranking porn sites shows dozens of videos of degrading treatment of women, an innocent person viewing it would think that is what sex is like. That is why it's so important that parents don't leave it too long to talk about porn.

WHAT YOU MIGHT BE THINKING

You may be angry and worried that what's been seen can't be unseen, shattering your child's innocence. You may also worry about how to explain what they saw, along with how it may affect them.

WHAT THEY MIGHT BE THINKING

◉ **Your tween is likely to have felt shocked and frightened** by some of the acts they saw, especially if they have been told up to now that sex is something that two people who love each other do to make a baby.

◉ **They may be confused by the violence they saw** and some of the expressions of pain, as well as the depictions of "school girls" having sex with adults. They may also be wondering why their developing bodies bear little resemblance to the exaggerated and enlarged body parts of people that appear in the most frequently viewed porn videos.

◉ **Your child may think women want to be treated like this**— landing pages will show shots of women looking happy to go along with degrading acts—when in reality they are being paid to or may have been sex trafficked.

◉ **Your tween may have felt their body reacting,** as porn is designed to be arousing, so they may feel ashamed and confused.

◉ **They may blame themself for inflicting this image on themself** if they clicked on a link because they were curious, or kept on watching.

HOW YOU COULD RESPOND

In the moment

Stay calm
Thank your child for telling you, because most tweens don't mention it, and you want your child to feel able to talk to you. Deal with any feelings of shock and anger first, and tell them they are not in trouble. Getting angry will only add to any trauma, confusion, or shame your child is feeling. The best way to reduce the impact of that is to give empathy and comfort.

Get the context
To respond in the best way, ask some gentle questions: How did it happen? Are they curious about sex? Did a friend, an older child, or adult show it to them? Did they see it at home or at school? Was this a one-off? Have they been watching it for a while?

Offer support
If they kept looking, let them know it's normal to be curious. Validate any feelings by saying: "My guess is what you saw was violent and shocking. I am always here to answer your questions."

Give some perspective
If your tween is squirming, tell them you'd like to talk to them for a fixed amount of time, say two minutes. Explain that what they saw was not the healthy, mutual, loving sex they can look forward to in a loving relationship when they grow up. Porn is a form of entertainment for some adults.

In the long term

Restrict access
Even if your child has already seen porn, check the settings on their gadgets to restrict access so it doesn't become a habit and cause serious damage to their sexual development.

Teach them to question it
The prevalence of porn and the lack of controls over it means the best protection for the teen years is teaching young people to ask questions about it. What messages does porn give about consent, gender roles, and race? What does it mean for women? What would it mean if everyone behaved like this? Who profits from it?

SEE RELATED TOPICS
I can fast-forward the bad parts: pp.126–127,
They asked me for a nude picture:
pp.194–195

"I'M SO TIRED"

As your child moves toward their teenage years, their sleep patterns will change. You may find they are awake later at night and find it harder to wake up in the mornings, especially if they're on screens at bedtime.

SCENARIO | Two hours after bedtime, you find your tween on their phone, secretly messaging friends. The next day they are very tired.

There are biological reasons for tweens wanting to stay up later than they once did. The hormone melatonin, which makes us feel sleepy, is released two to three hours later into the evening in adolescents than in children. Then, in the morning, the wake-up hormone cortisol is released later in adolescents, making it more difficult for them to get out of bed. School starting times remain the same, so a sleep deficit quickly builds up. Research shows that if sleep deprived, tweens find it harder to concentrate and remember what they've learned and may struggle to control their moods, impulses, and eating. Over time, this may lead to more challenging behavior, too.

WHAT YOU MIGHT BE THINKING

You're likely to be annoyed that your tween is hiding their late-night screen use, and frustrated that tiredness is likely to make them bad-tempered the next day.

WHAT THEY MIGHT BE THINKING

⊙ **Your tween might feel bedtime is their special time** to message friends, if they have lots of after-school activities and homework. They might prefer to be tired and lie to you than give up their "me time."

⊙ **Your tween may know they will have trouble waking up** the next day. But as their brains are wired toward immediate gratification and social connection, socializing online takes priority.

⊙ **They may not feel sleepy if they are looking at screens at bedtime,** as the blue light emitted by electronics interrupts the release of the sleep-inducing hormone melatonin.

⊙ **They may do everything from their bed,** from homework to watching TV shows, making it feel more like a flight deck than a place to sleep. If they are having trouble falling asleep, they may go to screens for entertainment.

◆ **SEE RELATED TOPICS** ◆
I'm old enough to stay up late!: pp.42–43
Can I go on a sleepover?: pp.82–83

HOW YOU COULD RESPOND

In the moment

Give them perspective
Let them know that while you appreciate they want to catch up with friends, sleep is key to well-being. The night is a peak time for disagreements to occur online. Explain that you'd like them to manage their phone by themselves, rather than insist on parental intervention.

Make the rules
Say that screens aren't allowed in bedrooms overnight. Research shows that children who have screens in their rooms overnight have more sleep problems, view more disturbing content, and have more difficult relationships.

Introduce a digital sunset
Work with them on a regular morning and evening routine. Set a good example and stop phone and screen use for everyone after a certain time. Make it a rule that all household screens are charged overnight outside your bedroom to show this is important for everyone.

In the long term

Present sleep as a health issue
Explain the biology of sleep and that it's just as important as food and exercise for healthy development. Sleep is also the main time when growth hormones are released and information is encoded in their brains. Frame screens as an interruption to an essential need. Explain how studies have found that a lack of sleep can make them less smart the next day.

Buy an alarm clock
Don't allow your child to use their phone as an alarm clock to justify keeping their phone in their bedroom at night.

Make them self-aware
Tweens are more likely to stick to bedtimes if they figure out for themselves why getting more sleep is good for them. Suggest they notice how short-tempered they are and how much more difficult it is to concentrate when they have stayed up late the night before.

"I **DARE** YOU!"

Tweens want to test their physical capabilities and impress their peers.
In addition, the area of the brain responsible for helping them plan
ahead and understand consequences isn't fully developed yet.
All of this helps to explain why tweens give each other dares.

SCENARIO | You overhear your tween daring their friend to try a dangerous social media challenge. You are concerned that they might come to harm.

Tweens are starting to take more risks to prove subconsciously that they can be independent and survive on their own. Research shows that in the ventral striatum, the area of the brain linked to reward, adolescents need more stimulation, novelty, and excitement to get the same "hit" as adults. One evolutionary theory is that putting themselves in more dangerous situations at this age prepares the younger members of the tribe to become more independent and exploratory, while still under the protection of grown-ups.

WHAT YOU MIGHT BE THINKING

If you've often told your tween to be careful, and they know about the injuries caused by challenges on the internet, you may be exasperated that they are planning such a prank.

> "
SUGGEST THEY TAKE A PAUSE AWAY FROM PEERS TO CHECK THEIR GUT FEELING.
"

WHAT THEY MIGHT BE THINKING

◉ **While your tween may realize what they are doing is risky,** the fact they are planning it with a friend will make it feel like the pros outweigh the cons.

◉ **Adolescent brains are wired to get more of a "kick"** from taking a risk than adult brains because it triggers more of the pleasure chemical dopamine.

◉ **It will feel like an invisible pull.** It's likely your tween won't be able to explain why they want to take risks.

◉ **Your tween's egocentricity** at this age has led to the creation of their own "personal fable," which leads them to believe they are invulnerable to harm.

HOW YOU COULD RESPOND

In the moment

Talk through scenarios
At home, ask your tween about the challenge, where they've seen it, what they know about it, and how they know that it wasn't staged online. Ask them to weigh up the pros and cons. Talk about how imagining a scenario with their friends can be just as rewarding because brain scans have found the anticipation of the risk is the most rewarding part.

Keep it in context
While it's nerve-racking for you, risk-taking serves a purpose. It allows your child to test themself and feel competent and resilient.

Talk about context
"Hot" contexts are when decisions are made in the heat of the moment, fueled by peer pressure, excitement, or a need for validation. "Cold" contexts are more logical decisions taken in the cold light of day. Suggest that they take a pause away from their peers to assess risky situations and give themself time to check their gut feeling.

In the long term

Ask "What if?"
You can help your child think about how to stand up to peer pressure by playing a friendly game of "What if?" Ask questions such as, "What if your friend dared you to jump from the top stair at school or dares you to drink three energy drinks in a row?" Let them ask questions, too, so they hear how you would handle a difficult situation.

Help them practice "no"
Suggest phrases they could use, such as: "This isn't my kind of thing," "Let's do something else instead," or just a clear "No, thanks." If they can't think of an excuse not to accept a dare, suggest they say, "My parents would kill me if I did this."

Explore safer risk-taking
Help your tween find other ways to take part in sensation-seeking, like mountain biking, rock climbing, or other outdoor sports. They can also take nonphysical risks, such as trying out for a role in the school play or running in a school election.

◤ **SEE RELATED TOPICS** ◢
Can I have a sip?: pp.168–169
I need new sneakers: pp.172–173

GENDER

A generation ago, parents assumed that their children would stay the same gender they were assigned at birth, either a boy or a girl. We now live in a world where gender is seen as a continuum and where people have more choice about how they identify.

Most people will stay with the gender they were assigned at birth, but some young people may decide they identify differently, or don't identify with any gender at all. While it may take some adjustment for you as a parent, keeping a strong connection with your child is essential. While they are deciding which direction to head in, view your role as accompanying them in the front seat. You may not be sure where they will go, but assure them you will travel alongside them.

1

Make equality a family value
However your tween's gender and sexuality develop, model equality with your co-parent in how you organize and run your home. Show your tween how to treat all human beings with respect and dignity. This will help tweens identify how they are feeling and take steps to manage their feelings.

"

USE THE NAME AND PRONOUNS THEY REQUEST. IT WILL BE IMPORTANT TO THEM THAT YOU RESPECT THEM.

WORKING THINGS OUT

6 key principles

2

Avoid gender stereotypes
In the tween years, children tend to accept the messages they get about gender without question. So avoid putting your child into traditional gender boxes with comments such as: "You're such a good girl" or "You're such a brave boy."

3

Understand the whole picture
Think of the different elements that add up to who your child is becoming: there's your child's biological sex, which is their sex organs at birth. Then there's their gender identity, which is what gender they feel. Then there is their sexual orientation.

4

Look at your own beliefs
Think about where you got your messages about what it means to be a man or a woman. Consider how these stereotypes can be restricting. Understanding how we're socialized to act in certain ways, according to the genitals we were born with, can help you understand any questioning by your child.

5

Be vigilant
Young people who don't fit into the accepted stereotypes of male and female are far more likely to be targeted for social cruelty. Keep a close eye on your child for any low mood, anxiety, and social withdrawal. Stay connected, asking what was positive and negative about their day and listen without judgment.

6

Respect names and pronouns
Your child's name may not reflect the gender they identify with now. So use the name and pronouns they request. Even if your child changes their mind later, it will be important to them that you respect them. It sends a message that you are prepared to accept whatever person your tween decides to be. Ask them if they want you to talk to the rest of the family or their school about any name or pronoun changes.

TAILORED ADVICE

8–10
YEARS OLD

Avoid gender norms
Give tweens a choice about what colors they want to wear or paint their rooms with, instead of offering pastels for daughters or dark colors for sons.

Support a gender mix
Encourage your child to have friends of all genders. Help them think about friends as the people they are rather than by gender.

Make rules equal
Avoid treating siblings differently according to their gender at birth and give them the same tasks around the house.

10–12
YEARS OLD

Take time to adjust
If your tween identifies as a different gender, it may be a challenge to rethink your expectations of their future. Give yourself time to adjust and seek support.

Avoid saying "It's a phase"
You may consider your child too young to know how they want to live, but accept that it's their choice to define who they are. Respect their views.

Support self-expression
Your tween is developing ways to present themself: support their choices in clothes and hair.

"I AM TELLING THE TRUTH"

There will be times when nearly all tweens lie, exaggerate, or leave out important details. By understanding the reason beneath these falsehoods, you can help prevent this from turning into a habit and have a more open and honest relationship with your child.

SCENARIO | Your child says they got 20/20 in a math test. At a parents' meeting, their teacher tells you this wasn't the case.

We tend to view lying as universally bad, but it helps to see it as a development point. There are two types of lies: antisocial lies are told to get out of trouble after wrongdoing, to escape punishment for breaking rules, or to put blame on others. Prosocial lies are untruths told by omitting information, rather than telling deliberate fibs. Children may tell these "white lies" to try to please you, impress others, or not cause hurt. Tweens will also try out lying to maintain a sense of independence and privacy. While not all lies are serious, if your tween tells them often to avoid what they need to do, get themself out of trouble, or look better in front of others, they will need your help to find better strategies.

WHAT YOU MIGHT BE THINKING

You may be tempted to punish them. You may also be baffled that they told a lie that could be found out so easily and worry that their lying reflects badly on you.

SEE RELATED TOPICS

Is Santa real?: pp.34–35
Nothing! It was just a normal day:
pp.116–117

WHAT THEY MIGHT BE THINKING

● **Tweens want to impress their parents**. They accept adult judgment without question. They may lie to save themselves the pain of disappointing you.

● **Your tween may experiment** to see whether their stories will be believed, even though they know lying is wrong. They may try out lies to increase status with peers, like claiming they are going to get a pony because they'd like that to be true.

● **Without the life experience or brain development to foresee** the consequences, tweens may use magical thinking to tell themselves you won't find out.

● **Your tween is figuring out ways to manage discomfort**. Lying so you are pleased with them feels good momentarily. When they are caught out, they may insist they are telling the truth because they are embarrassed.

HOW YOU COULD RESPOND

In the moment

Ask open questions
Calm yourself by first seeing the lie as an ineffective way for your tween to communicate how they are feeling about themself and their schoolwork. Get ready to talk to them in a way that will make them feel safe to tell the truth in the future.

Be curious
You could say something like: "I understand that you wanted to do well and it might have hurt when you didn't. Honesty is important and I want to be able to trust you in the future. Can you come and talk to me or your teacher next time you feel this way, so we can help you prepare for the test?" If they continue to lie, say something like: "It sounds like you're finding it hard to be honest, but it's always easier when you are."

Explain your perspective
Say you are more upset with the fact that they lied than the fact that they got a bad grade, because you want to have an honest relationship with them. Assure your tween you love them for who they are, not for what they achieve.

In the long term

Help your child
If tweens are lying to build themselves up, it's a sign they don't feel good enough about themselves as they are. If your child finds schoolwork hard, find other activities in their lives at which they naturally do well. Feeling competent in other areas will help boost their self-worth. Speak to their teachers about any learning challenges.

Watch for an escalation
If your tween is lying a lot more than usual, it could be a sign that something else is going on. Spend extra time together to find out how they are feeling and what might lie beneath it. Do they feel under pressure to achieve a lot at school? Do they feel overwhelmed and find it hard to concentrate? Talk it through so they can discuss their worries. Tackle the cause of the problem.

Explain consequences
Help them learn from this. Whatever their reason, explain lies are wrong. Talk about how lying is complicated and stressful to maintain and prevents others from being able to give help when they need it. Then, every time your tween communicates honestly, notice and appreciate it.

❝ ❞

SAY YOU ARE MORE UPSET WITH THE FACT THAT THEY LIED THAN THE FACT THAT THEY GOT A BAD GRADE, BECAUSE YOU WANT TO HAVE AN HONEST RELATIONSHIP WITH THEM.

"CAN I HAVE **A SIP?**"

To your tween, alcohol looks like a mysterious magic potion that grown-ups drink to relax and have fun. Now that they consider themself older, they may be curious to taste it to find out why it's so valued by adults.

SCENARIO | At dinnertime, your tween asks if they can have a sip of the wine you're drinking.

Many parents believe that introducing young people to alcohol at home will train them to drink responsibly. But research has found that those given a drink by the age of 11 are up to four times more likely to binge-drink when older and are more likely to drink more overall. Furthermore, the effects of drinking on the developing brain—in particular, the areas that govern learning and memory—can be more serious and longer-lasting than previously thought. So, at this stage, when tweens are open to taking on your values, it's worth educating them about the effects of alcohol.

WHAT YOU MIGHT BE THINKING

You may think it's funny watching their reaction to the taste and that it's better for them to sample it first at home than binge-drink when they are older.

WHAT THEY MIGHT BE THINKING

⊙ **Your tween will have seen how alcohol is prized as a treat**, used to celebrate occasions, and will be curious about why.

⊙ **They may want to try it to see how it tastes**, and whether it affects how they feel, given that adults like it so much.

⊙ **Your tween knows alcohol is off-limits** for children, so it feels daring and grown-up to give it a try.

⊙ **Your tween may wrongly assume that it's always safe** to drink if they have seen you do it, not realizing how it can affect their health and decision-making when it's taken in larger doses.

" "

MAKE YOUR TWEEN AWARE OF MOCKTAILS AND SPECIAL FIZZY DRINKS AS AN ALTERNATIVE.

◀ **SEE RELATED TOPICS** ▶
I dare you!: pp.162–163
You can't tell me what to eat!: pp.182–183

HOW YOU COULD RESPOND

In the moment

Make it a health issue
Talk about how studies show even moderate, regular drinking can interfere with a critical stage in the development of children's brains and cause long-term memory loss. Discuss how scientists say that it's not totally safe to drink until the brain has fully matured at around the age of 25, so the longer they leave it to start drinking alcohol, the better. You could say something like: "Your brain is still developing and we don't want anything to interrupt that. So, at the moment, we're going to play it safe."

Start the conversation
Now your child is curious, take the opportunity to start talking over the coming years about the importance of drinking moderately—and in a safe context. Rather than sit them down for a big talk, keep chatting about alcohol as their questions, real-life situations, and news stories come up.

In the long term

Be a good role model
Studies show that children tend to copy their drinking habits from their parents. Avoid portraying alcohol as a coping mechanism for stress, an essential way to unwind after a long day, or a must-have if you want to have fun with friends. While trying to set a good example, don't see your own drinking as a barrier to talking about the health risk of booze for your child.

Set out your values
Talk about the pros and cons of alcohol. Explain that while alcohol can taste nice and be relaxing, it's also a drug for use in moderate amounts and it can affect decision-making, which is why it's illegal for those under the age of 18. Make your tween aware of mocktails and special fizzy drinks as an alternative.

Discuss future challenges
Talk to your tween about how, when they are older, they will feel the pressure to drink more, and alcohol is more likely to impair their judgment in less predictable situations, putting their health and safety at risk. However, make it clear that while you'd like them to leave drinking alcohol as late as possible, you will always be there to help them if they drink too much and become vulnerable.

"HOW TALL WILL I GET?"

Tweens grow at different rates. Whether they've shot up ahead of their peers, or are lagging a little behind the average, height can affect how they feel about themselves and can impact their place in their peer groups.

SCENARIO | Your tween is one of the shorter students in their class when they start middle school and they are concerned they may never be tall.

As girls start puberty first, they grow on average one to two years before boys, spurting up from the age of 9 or 10, stopping around two years after their periods start. Boys' growth spurts are likely to start around two years later, from the age of 12, until they are 16. This means that when boys start middle school, there may be a lot of girls taller than them. All healthy tweens who get the nutrients they need will reach their genetically predetermined heights eventually. But because height is associated with power, strength, and masculinity, a boy's height can be a preoccupation until then.

WHAT YOU MIGHT BE THINKING

You may worry that your son looks too young to stand up for himself at middle school and that he will get bullied, especially if his sport uniform swamps him.

WHAT THEY MIGHT BE THINKING

⊚ **To tween boys, size equals authority.** If they start middle school on the shorter side, they may find they miss out on social status.

⊚ **Shorter boys may feel less masculine and more intimidated** when they start middle school, unless they have a confident persona or a good sense of humor. Research shows that shorter boys are more at risk of being bullied, so they may try to compensate by acting tougher and more aggressively.

⊚ **Shorter tween boys may feel frustrated** if they are starting to develop sexual feelings and they get overlooked, and treated as cute, by taller girls who might be attracted to more mature-looking classmates.

⊚ **Girls may not be as bothered as boys about staying smaller** as it's construed as cute and feminine. However, their stature may determine their friendship group at the start of middle school because older-looking, more grown-up-looking girls will tend to stick together.

◀ **SEE RELATED TOPICS** ▶
When will I get my period?: pp.148–149
What's happening to my voice?: pp.154–155

HOW YOU COULD RESPOND

In the moment

Listen to them
Don't laugh off their concerns or tell them to be patient. Empathize and reassure them: "That sounds tough and I hear you are frustrated that you are not yet as tall as some of the other children your age. I can't fix this because growth is directed by hormones, so the best we can do is make sure you get all the nutrients you need and sleep the hours you need—and I will always be here to listen."

Give the bigger picture
Assure your child that growth can come in fits and starts and, while it's impossible to control, they will reach the height they were meant to be eventually. If they are interested, show them photos of yourself and your co-parent at different heights as you grew up to illustrate that they will get there, just as you have. Explain that it will all even out and though they may start growing later, they may keep growing for longer.

In the long term

Help them adapt
Talk about how posture can reflect confidence. Tell them around 75 percent of communication is nonverbal, so how we move, stand, walk, and talk will convey confidence and maturity. Speaking clearly and keeping eye contact are also important. Role-play how different postures look to show how they affect demeanor. Explain we'd all rather spend time with someone funny, kind, and interesting, of any size, than a tall person who is none of these things.

Change the focus
Make sure your tween feels valued for other qualities. Encourage shorter tweens to take part in activities or clubs where height is not a factor, such as chess, or where shorter stature may be an advantage, such as gymnastics or dance.

Don't tease
Avoid labeling your tween according to their size with nicknames, or by making jokes about it, as this will make them feel more self-conscious.

❝ ❞

ENCOURAGE THEM TO TAKE PART IN CLUBS WHERE HEIGHT IS NOT A FACTOR.

"I NEED NEW SNEAKERS"

As they become more status-orientated, your tween may ask for designer shoes, bags, and clothes, which they believe will help them fit in or impress their peers. You may be torn between wanting them to belong and wanting to hold on to your hard-earned cash.

SCENARIO | Your tween asks for a pair of $250 trainers, saying that "all their friends" have them.

Your tween may be seeking to signal their belonging to their new "tribe" of peers by wearing the same types of clothes. Within friendship groups, there will be unwritten rules about how members dress, which makes your tween feel it's essential to get it "right."

Footwear is considered especially important, particularly for boys who tend to have fewer ways of expressing themselves through clothes. But as sneakers are functional and sporty, designer versions may feel okay for boys to covet.

WHAT YOU MIGHT BE THINKING

You may feel annoyed that your tween wants only an expensive brand when their feet are growing fast. You may worry that if you don't buy them, they will feel left out. It may trigger memories of wanting to belong.

WHAT THEY MIGHT BE THINKING

◉ **Your tween wants these shoes to say: "I belong too."** They may also believe this show-of affluence will give them status in their social hierarchy at school.

◉ **Your tween may now be exposed to more ads** on social media, but may not yet have developed the ability to question the messages. They may simply believe the sneakers will make them look as cool as the people in the ad.

◉ **Tweens don't just want the "right" sneakers to belong.** They also want them as "insurance" against getting the wrong ones and being made fun of by their friends.

◉ **They may insist "everyone else has these shoes,"** when in fact only a few high-status males in their social group do. But they still want to look like them, believing they will get the same social respect by having the same shoes.

◆ **SEE RELATED TOPICS** ◆
All my friends have a phone: pp.62–63
I didn't think you'd mind: pp.74–75

" "
COULD THEY WAIT FOR A SALE, SELL SOMETHING, OR EARN THE MONEY?

HOW YOU COULD RESPOND

In the moment

Empathize
Consider your child's request. If the answer is no, say you understand it is frustrating, but you are concerned about spending this much on shoes that may not fit for long.

Brainstorm solutions
If your tween is still insistent, could they find a pair on a second-hand website? Could they wait for a sale, Christmas, or their next birthday, sell something, or earn the money? This will help them learn firsthand that things feel better when they work hard to buy them.

Look for a middle way
Explain that while you will buy them everything they need, you can't afford everything they want—and there's a difference. If your tween really does need a new pair of shoes, you could agree to give them the money for a basic pair and suggest they make up the difference themself.

In the long term

Avoid bigging up brands
Children pick up ideas about money from overhearing their parents' "money scripts," which reveal attitudes to spending. Avoid coveting brands yourself and make it clear they are as much about perception as reality.

Bring up budgeting
Discuss how you make decisions about money, and the invisible costs you have to meet, like taxes. Talk about how if you spend more on one item, you have less cash for other things, and how many hours you worked for it.

Chat about consumerism
When adolescents learn how they are being manipulated by marketing, they become more resistant. Help your child recognize persuasive techniques and messages that products can "fix" problems or make people more important. Talk about where products are manufactured, the conditions and pay of the workers, and price mark-ups.

"THEY'RE JUST SCRATCHES"

As social and academic pressure builds, some tweens try self-harm
as a way to deal with overwhelming feelings. Understandably,
this can be very distressing for a parent and something
you feel unprepared for.

SCENARIO | You have spotted some cuts on the inside of your child's
arm and are worried they are hurting themselves.

Tweens self-harm for several reasons. It may be
a way to distract from emotional pain, a release
valve for strong feelings, or a way to make
their pain visible to parents, teachers, or
peers. All genders can self-harm, and it
can take the form of anything that causes
deliberate pain, from self-bruising, to biting
and burning. It does not mean tweens are
trying to kill themselves. Rather it's a way to
be in control when everything else feels out
of control. However, if tweens go on to find
that self-harm gives them relief, they may
keep returning to it, creating a vicious cycle.

WHAT YOU MIGHT
BE THINKING

**You may feel shocked, angry,
and confused** that your child
would want to hurt themselves.
You may feel in a constant state
of vigilance, aware that they
might do it again.

WHAT THEY MIGHT BE THINKING

⦿ **Your tween may have had a fallout with a friend** or family member, or they may be feeling lonely and worthless. All these are common triggers for self-harming for the first time.

⦿ **If they know others who have self-harmed** in their year group, they may experiment with it to see how it feels.

⦿ **Tweens are prone to black-and-white thinking.** Your child may be causing themselves physical pain they can control to see if it detracts from the emotional pain they can't. In the moment, the pain in their bodies takes away from the pain in their heads.

⦿ **As they compare themself at secondary school** in everything from academics to looks and popularity, your tween may feel they should punish themself for not being "good enough" if they feel they are falling short.

◆ **SEE RELATED TOPICS** ◆
I am telling the truth: pp.166–167
I didn't mean to punch the wall: pp.176–177

HOW YOU COULD RESPOND

In the moment

Help them open up
Encourage your child to talk. Say something like: "When someone feels cross or sad, they can want to hurt themself to release feelings. I have seen marks on your arm and am worried because they look deliberate. There are a lot of reasons people do that. Is this something you'd ever do?" Unless there is another obvious way they could have hurt themself, trust your instincts.

Be open to talking
Self-harm stirs up complex feelings. You may feel you have failed your child but are desperate to avoid doing anything that would trigger more self-harm. Take self-harm seriously, as a sign your tween is communicating their distress. If your tween denies it, tell them you are always ready to talk.

Stay calm
If your tween opens up, assure them of your unconditional love. If you are in shock, simply say: "I don't yet understand how you feel, but I'm so glad you told me." Seek support so you are in a better position to support them.

In the long term

Spend time together
Invite your tween to spend more time with you, instead of leaving them to ruminate in their bedroom. Find opportunities for fun one-on-one time together, with no judgment, to reassure them of your unconditional love.

Suggest alternatives
To break the cycle, your tween will need to notice when feelings build and find ways to cope. Ways to feel "harmless pain" include squeezing an ice cube, drawing on skin, cold showers, or eating a hot chili. Suggest other tactics to express their feelings in the moment, such as talking to a safe person, writing, calling a helpline, or doing an activity outside.

Talk about consequences
When the body is injured, it produces endorphins, a natural pain reliever giving temporary relief. Help tweens understand that it isn't an effective coping method long term as it feeds into shame, risks health, and can scar.

Talk freely in neutral spaces
Give them opportunities to talk freely, ideally outside in neutral spaces. Stress there is nothing wrong with feeling anxiety and anger. When these surge, talk about riding a wave that will pass.

"I DIDN'T MEAN TO PUNCH THE WALL"

Helping a child learn how to calm down from a bout of anger and cope with difficult feelings in a healthy way is one of the most important jobs we will ever do as parents.

SCENARIO | When you take away your tween's game console, you are shocked that they punch the wall in anger, hurting themselves.

At every age, feelings of anger are triggered by frustration, fear, disappointment, or sadness. We get better at controlling the feelings that result as we get older. But as tweens enter puberty, outbursts can be common as they face frustrations and are flooded with hormones, such as testosterone, which can contribute to aggression. These tantrums look similar to those they had as toddlers, but because tweens are bigger and more physically powerful, the outbursts are scarier to deal with.

WHAT YOU MIGHT BE THINKING

You may be shocked at the intensity of your child's anger and, if it happens often, you might be on tenterhooks waiting for their next outburst.

SEE RELATED TOPICS
I didn't hit them: pp.70–71
They're just scratches: pp.174–175

WHAT THEY MIGHT BE THINKING

⊚ **Boys experience big emotions** when they go through adrenarche, which is a rise in the release of hormones from the adrenal glands, in preparation for the hormonal onslaught of puberty. Research has found they may become emotionally reactive at this time.

⊚ **Your child knows they should not act violently,** but in the moment, they are overwhelmed by their feelings and don't know how to stop them.

⊚ **The alarm system in your tween's emotional brain** is extremely reactive. So when its threat detector, the amygdala, is triggered, it sparks the release of adrenaline and cortisol into their nervous system before their rational brain kicks in.

⊚ **Your child wants to feel safe and back in control.** They may also feel ashamed and confused because the aggressive behavior is at odds with your usual loving relationship.

HOW YOU COULD RESPOND

In the moment

Handle it like a tantrum
When your child is overwhelmed to this extent, their emotional centers are in charge, and they are unlikely to process anything you say to reason with them. Instead, help your tween take deep breaths, focusing particularly on the exhale, to calm their nervous system.

Acknowledge feelings
You could say: "It looks like you were really upset that I took your console and you had a lot of difficult feelings trying to get out, including frustration and anger." Naming their feelings will help them deal with them.

Reconnect later
Show you care and reconnect by checking that they have not hurt themself badly when they punched the wall. When you both feel ready, later in the day, ask them if they want a hug.

In the long term

Focus on well-being
Make sure your child gets plenty of sleep and regular healthy meals and exercise. Otherwise, their system may be more reactive.

Anger versus aggression
Tell your tween there's nothing wrong with feeling angry, but we all need safe ways to express it, to avoid scaring or hurting others or ourselves. At a neutral time, talk in third person about the difference between anger, which is healthy, and aggression, which is not.

Make them self-aware
Show them how to spot signs that their nervous system is being activated when they get angry, such as an increasing heart rate, sweaty palms, or muscle clenching, so they can take steps to calm it down. This could include grounding techniques, such as deep breathing, counting from 1 to 20, or clenching and unclenching their fists. Help them visualize anger as a volcano about to blow and to notice the signs when the lava is rising. Or they could imagine it as a carbonated drink bottle that, shaken up, will explode when opened. But if the bubbles are allowed to settle and the top is opened slowly, the same feelings can seep out gradually.

Be a role model
The best way to teach emotional regulation is by modeling it yourself. Express your feelings when you feel angry or sad, but demonstrate the safer ways you have of dealing with them, such as assertive communication, confiding in a friend, or writing down angry thoughts.

" "

HELP THEM VISUALIZE ANGER AS A VOLCANO AND TO NOTICE WHEN THE LAVA IS RISING.

THE **DIGITAL** WORLD

As tweens start to use screens, the digital world can become the number-one worry for parents. Remember that they use the digital world to do the same things we did at their age: play games and chat with friends.

It is worrying for parents because tweens are doing these activities in spaces designed and populated by grown-ups. For many tweens, their understanding of the world is not developed enough to foresee the risks. Your guidance is vital because there is so much for them to navigate. While they are still developing critical thinking skills, emotional intelligence, decision-making, judgment, and perspective, it's important that you curate their experience. This includes restricting their activity to private groups of close friends, setting up safety and privacy settings, and helping to choose the websites, apps, and search engines they use.

1

Set a good example
Be a good role-model with your own digital use and set aside time with your tween when you are not on your phone. Talk through how you set limits and how you know you need a break.

4

Introduce a digital sunset
If your child has use of a tablet or console, set a rule of no screens for an hour before bedtime as they can emit sleep-disrupting light.

6

Have screen-free times
Keep coming-home times, mealtimes, and days out tech-free so that devices don't interrupt family life. Frame screen-free time spent together as a reward, not a punishment.

WORKING THINGS OUT

8 key principles

2

Keep talking

Explore the online world together and ask your child about what they're seeing. Stay connected so they come to you for advice and reassurance first, rather than going onto social media.

3

Stick to the "golden hour"

Research suggests that the more time adolescents spend online alone, the more likely they are to get caught up in cyberbullying. Experts believe an hour a day for adolescents is long enough to keep up with peers but short enough to avoid conflict.

5

Show how to use tech actively

Use technology to learn, create, and connect with your child, rather than just for passive entertainment. This could mean taking photos, doing online projects, or recording videos together. Don't give up on teaching them real-world activities, such as writing letters, doing crafts, outdoor skills, and cooking.

7

Think of it as a health issue

In the same way that eating chips and cookies all day wouldn't make us feel well, talk about how spending most of our time on screens also wouldn't help us feel well. Ask your tween to notice signs that they have had enough.

8

Stay in charge

Tweens can be vocal about what they want, but remember you have the experience, maturity, common sense, and wisdom they don't yet have. There's little evidence that children lose out socially if they don't have a phone before middle school.

TAILORED ADVICE

8–10
YEARS OLD

Delay

The sooner you give your tween a phone, the harder you will work to make sure they stay safe using it.

Use the big screen

Restrict your tween to going online on a family computer or TV screen in common areas of your home, never in bedrooms.

Keep it basic

If they need a phone (perhaps with a co-parent living elsewhere) provide a "dumb phone" that only sends messages and makes calls. Avoid sophisticated devices at this stage.

10–12
YEARS OLD

Make it private

Tell tweens to stick to private group chats rather than posting on social media for now. Show them how to block and report.

Underline the basics

Remind them of the bottom line: never say anything to someone online that you wouldn't say to their face.

Give a pause button

As social conflict rises, give a mantra to remind them not to react quickly. Try: "When emotions are high, keep actions low."

"AM I **FAT?**"

As children go through puberty, their bodies will change. Now that tweens grow up surrounded by more images of so-called "ideal" bodies, they may start criticizing how theirs compares, even before they have stopped growing.

SCENARIO | Your child becomes angry when trying on clothes for a party and claims nothing fits. When you ask what's wrong, they say: "Am I fat?"

Tweens are caught at a difficult crossroad. On one hand, they are growing up in a world that confers status on those with so-called "perfect bodies." At the same time, they may spend less time exercising and more time sitting down, due to increased screen time. Furthermore, they also live in a society where a wide range of heavily processed foods have never been so readily available. As tweens start to make their own food choices, but also compare their appearance, they may question if their body is "good enough," even while it's still going through important and necessary changes.

WHAT YOU MIGHT BE THINKING

You may worry that if you say the wrong thing, you could damage their self-image and tip them toward unhealthy eating. You may feel guilty if you've had these thoughts about your own body.

WHAT THEY MIGHT BE THINKING

⊚ **Your tween may be feeling anxious or rejected** for other reasons but processing these feelings as discomfort with their bodies. They may believe they would be more admired by their peers if they had the "ideal" body shape.

⊚ **Your child may be comparing themselves unconsciously** to adult celebrities and influencers, forgetting that they are still children who have not yet finished growing.

⊚ **Girls put on up to 20 percent body fat during puberty,** but may wrongly see this change as "putting on weight."

⊚ **Your tween may be venting frustration,** seeking reassurance, and wanting you to say no but then dismiss your words because you're their parent.

◀ **SEE RELATED TOPICS** ▶
I want a makeover party: pp.86–87
I'm not pretty enough: pp.104–105

HOW YOU COULD RESPOND

In the moment

Listen to them
Your first instinct may be to rush to deny that they are fat. Instead listen, acknowledge their feelings, and resist the temptation to agree or disagree. Brain scientists believe that uncontradicted, a strong feeling can fade in just 90 seconds. Instead, you could say: "It sounds like it's difficult to choose an outfit. Are you worried about anything else at the moment?"

Offer a hug
After listening, let them know you think they are lovely as they are. Your reassurance and unconditional love will give them comfort.

In the long term

Talk about puberty
Explain that at this age their body is changing from a child's to a grown-up's. It can take a long time and during this transition stage, their body can feel unfamiliar.

Explain feelings versus facts
At another time when your tween is not upset, you could talk about how body image is not based on reality but on our emotional state. It can be influenced by mood, worries, and recent experiences. While they might believe that the problem is their appearance, the real problem is their thoughts about how they look. Emphasize that "feeling fat" is a feeling, not a fact.

Discuss "fat talk"
"Fat talk" is a term coined by body image researchers to describe how people criticize their bodies. Talk about why it's wrong to use the word "fat" as an insult and to notice how they and others talk about their bodies—this helps them become aware of how unhelpful it is.

Talk about balance
Show how a varied diet is part of a well-rounded package of self-care, including sleep and exercise, that adds up to feeling well. Explain that no food is off limits, but some are treats, rather than essentials, and an active lifestyle helps all bodies be fitter.

Check social media
Be curious about your child's social media interests. What are they feeding their minds? Ask if they'd feel better unfollowing any accounts that make them feel "not good enough." Suggest that your tween curates social media feeds toward accounts for social causes or interests that aren't to do with physical appearance.

> **THE REAL PROBLEM IS THEIR THOUGHTS ABOUT HOW THEY LOOK.**

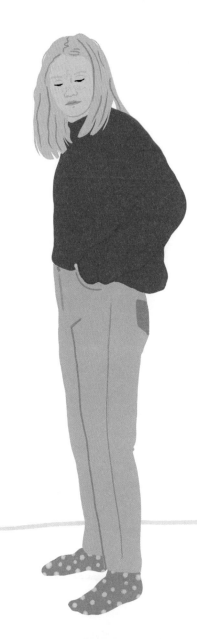

"YOU CAN'T TELL ME WHAT TO EAT!"

When you child was smaller, as a parent, you had control over what your child ate. Now that they have more independence and want to choose for themselves, you may worry about the decisions they make about food.

SCENARIO | Your tween is sitting on the sofa eating crisps and you question if they should be snacking on so much "junk".

Rising rates of obesity mean that we worry far more about what our kids eat than we used to. Although it comes from a place of love and concern, trying to control our children's diet can backfire. As tweens now have more autonomy over their diet, eating the foods that you try to limit can become a way of rebelling against your authority and become a battle of wills you can't win. By demonizing certain foods and making them feel forbidden, you may inadvertently make them more attractive.

WHAT YOU MIGHT BE THINKING

You may be annoyed to see your tween eating chips just before dinnertime and fear that unless you put some boundaries around their food choices, they will just eat sugar and processed foods all the time.

WHAT THEY MIGHT BE THINKING

◉ **Tweens crave high-calorie foods, and after a long day** at school, they feel they deserve a "treat." They may also be eating out of habit because they are bored, or stressed, or for a short-term mood boost.

◉ **Now that they are coming home from middle school on their own,** your tween may love the newfound freedom of being able to buy their own snacks with their pocket money. It may also help them bond with friends after school.

◉ **Now that your tween can make more of their own food choices,** eating candy and chips that you once tried to limit when they were little may be their way of enjoying their growing independence.

◉ **Once they've opened a new packet, they may mindlessly** keep going until they are finished if they don't check how their body feels, especially if they are on a screen and too distracted to pay attention to signals from their body that they have had enough.

◤ **SEE RELATED TOPICS** ◢
I'm turning vegan: pp.192–193
I'm doing a glow-up challenge: pp.196–197

HOW YOU COULD RESPOND

In the moment

Hold your judgment
Parents who don't comment on their children's food choices at this age have kids with more balanced eating habits. Rather than criticize your tween when you see them snacking, point out that you are happy they are treating themselves but let them know what time you will be having dinner. If they are rude, make it clear you don't appreciate their tone and remove yourself from the situation so as not to get pulled into a conflict.

Keep perspective
Your tween is growing fast, so it's normal for them to crave more calories as well as gain some weight during puberty. Such treats are fine to eat if your child is exercising and eating them as part of a balanced diet.

In the long term

Teach them fullness
At mealtimes, ask yourself and the rest of the family questions such as, "Have you had enough?" and "Do you feel full?" so they get into the habit of noticing their body's fullness signals.

Talk neutrally about foods
Every food is okay in moderation. Avoid labeling foods as "good" and "healthy" or "bad" and "junk," which implies a moral choice and that the person eating them is bad. You could use the terms "anytime" and "sometimes" foods. Avoid talking about calories and weight loss and refer to having energy and feeling well.

Involve them
Ask your child to come shopping with you to choose snacks at the more nourishing end of the spectrum. See if they would like to help with your online food order or pick out a recipe they'd like to make with you so they are involved in the food process and realize it can be creative and fun.

Give them control
Make it clear that your role as a parent has always been to provide them with a balance of foods to meet their body's nutritional and energy needs so that they grow. Explain it's now becoming their responsibility to choose foods that will make them fit and strong.

Eat together as a family
Studies show that eating together encourages children to eat well and keeps you connected. Food becomes an experience to enjoy rather than a stress. If you reduce uncertainty around meal timings, tweens are also less likely to reach for snacks.

"WHY CAN'T I WEAR MASCARA TO SCHOOL?"

Your tween may want to wear makeup to school as a way of trying to fit in with her peers. Even a small amount of makeup may make her feel more confident and grown-up.

SCENARIO | Your tween is late setting off for school because she wants to apply mascara and lip gloss, despite it being against the rules.

For many tweens, wearing makeup is a fun way to experiment with different looks, but it can also become a way of conforming (or not) to what they believe society expects. Encouraging tweens to question and understand why they want to wear makeup will help them become more aware of the decisions they are making, as well as how much time and money they want to invest in cosmetics in years to come.

WHAT YOU MIGHT BE THINKING

You may be annoyed that your daughter is stressing over her appearance and concerned that she will get into trouble at school for wearing makeup.

" "
IF YOUR CHILD IS OVERAPPLYING MAKEUP, CONSIDER GETTING ADVICE AT A COSMETICS COUNTER.

WHAT THEY MIGHT BE THINKING

● **Using cosmetics may be a bonding activity** if your tween is friends with a socially sophisticated group of girls who have started wearing makeup.

● **She may avoid activities that risk her makeup fading.** Research shows some adolescent girls avoid getting hot and sweaty in school sports for this reason.

● **Although she may feel more confident wearing makeup,** your tween may start feeling exposed, vulnerable, or "not pretty enough" without it and may spend break times reapplying.

● **Your tween may be applying more makeup then she needs** if she is copying makeup vloggers. Vloggers are given free products by cosmetic companies, so they add these extra products into their online routines.

HOW YOU COULD RESPOND

In the moment

Be curious
Ask your tween why it's important. Without shaming her, ask why she likes putting on makeup. What features is she hoping to emphasize with cosmetics, and why? Do her friends also wear makeup to school?

Get her thinking
Ask why she thinks the school has banned makeup. Is it because girls her age don't need it? Is it because it's expensive and time-consuming? Is she willing to get into trouble with teachers? Encourage your tween to weigh up the pros and cons.

Avoid banning it
If you try to stop your daughter from wearing makeup, she is likely to apply it secretly. Understand that she might want to experiment, but emphasize that she will still be attractive whether she wears it or not. Be reassured that studies show that for many girls, preoccupation with makeup is a passing phase.

In the long term

Focus on skincare
Address underlying issues, such as acne, if she is self-conscious and trying to cover it up with make-up. Remind her that she has the young complexion that older generations miss in later life, so you'd like to help her enjoy it.

Give guidance
If your child is overapplying it, do an online tutorial together. They may wear less if they are more skilled at applying it. Encourage the use of products that enhance and protect rather than cover, like SPF moisturizer and lip balm.

Say it's not a cure-all
Explain that beauty comes from a healthy, fresh-faced look achieved by eating a balanced diet, exercising, and sleeping well. Say everyone has unique features that they can bring out with make-up, but cosmetics don't make you who you are.

Start conversations
Chat about how beauty standards have changed through the ages: women once covered their faces in white lead. Discuss animal testing and how makeup is one of the most expensive commodities.

◄ **SEE RELATED TOPICS** ►
I want a makeover party: pp.86–87
I'm not pretty enough: pp.104–105

"IT'S NOT **MY JOB**"

It can be tricky to know what to expect of your child when it comes to doing chores, but keep in mind that being given responsibilities at home can help tweens become more competent and independent.

SCENARIO | When you ask your tween to unload the dishwasher, they say it's not their job.

The amount of time kids spend helping parents at home has fallen rapidly over recent generations. As kids have more homework and extracurricular activities, parents expect them to do fewer chores. Furthermore, they won't feel as house-proud as you and may not "see" mess you refer to. They are also developing an understanding of cause and effect—what happens if tasks are left undone. As they tend to take for granted care from grown-ups, and mainly see the world from their point of view, they may need help to see it's time to pitch in.

WHAT YOU MIGHT BE THINKING

If you're at the end of your rope, you're likely to feel resentful and annoyed. You may be wondering why you're cleaning up after your child as if they are a toddler.

WHAT THEY MIGHT BE THINKING

◉ **Your tween may feel that they are entitled to "chill"** if homework and extracurricular activities take up a lot of their time. If you continue to do everything for them, they will see no reason to change.

◉ **They may fill their spare time going online** if they have access to a tablet or phone. Being abruptly asked to step away to do real-world activities, with no immediate gratification, will feel like a wrench that they may resent.

◉ **Your tween may have figured out that if they do chores badly** enough, or only after a lot of arguments, you'll give up asking because it's easier and quicker for you to do it yourself.

◉ **Your tween may genuinely believe that homework** is their only "job," as you've probably put so much emphasis on the importance of their schoolwork.

HOW YOU COULD RESPOND

In the moment

Ask them when
If they say they can't do a chore now, ask them when. Offering a choice will make them more likely to follow through. When they complete the task, thank them.

Time it
Give them an idea of how long it will take, or put a timer on and make it a race. If a task takes 15 minutes, add 15 minutes to their bedtime as a thank you.

Talk about teamwork
Describe your family as a machine with moving parts. Everyone must do their part for it to run smoothly. Choose a household mantra, such as "Family gets it done."

In the long term

Make tasks fun
Tweens can avoid chores they see as boring. If you make tasks fun, they will be less of a burden. If you have a weekly chore, like ironing and folding laundry, make it a date to chat and put on music. The more bonding the chore is, the less your tween will resist.

Give training
Tweens can feel overwhelmed the first time they are asked to do a job. Without shaming, say: "Let's do it together" and show them step by step. Make it feel fun for younger tweens in the kitchen by giving them a chef's hat or apron.

Don't expect perfection
Tweens are more likely to dodge a task if they think you won't think it's good enough. Encourage them to get started on small tasks, so they start to feel competent and as if they are making a contribution.

See chores as a life skill
We tend to focus on our children's academic achievements, but getting them to do chores is a better predictor of success and teaches them self-reliance, self-worth, and responsibility. See giving them chores as an investment in their future.

SEE RELATED TOPICS
Don't tell me what to do!: pp.118–119
You can't tell me what to eat!: pp.182–183

❝ ❞

IF A TASK TAKES 15 MINUTES, ADD 15 MINUTES TO THEIR BEDTIME AS A THANK YOU.

"IT'S ONLINE SO IT MUST BE TRUE"

Tweens are curious and eager to figure out how the world works. With the internet so readily available to them, they have a powerful tool for finding out. However, it's key that your tween learns to ask questions about the sources of information and its accuracy.

SCENARIO | Your tween has seen a clip that claims their favorite TV show predicted a major news event and is eager to share it with you.

As your tween's world view is expanding, the obvious place for them to turn to find out more is the internet. Now that families no longer gather around the same television set to consume news, tweens often pick up their information from multiple sources on their own on laptops, tablets, and phones. This can mean they are getting their information without the benefit of a more experienced adult perspective, and they may be led down rabbit holes that give them unbalanced views.

WHAT YOU MIGHT BE THINKING

Your immediate reaction may be to laugh off your tween's discovery. At the same time, you may worry about what other false news they will be taken in by.

◆ **SEE RELATED TOPICS** ◆
My selfie got 100 likes!: pp.140–141
My friend showed me this video on their phone: pp.158–159

WHAT THEY MIGHT BE THINKING

⊚ **As tweens are surrounded by adults** who they believe have a responsibility to tell the truth, they don't understand that some adults seek to manipulate or trick others for their own ends.

⊚ **As your tween does not yet question adult authority,** they have not developed the confidence to question information that, to them, looks official.

⊚ **Conspiracy theories may appeal** to a tween's desire to make sense of the world. They can access information that will entertain peers and feel like they know more than others.

⊚ **If your tween has clicked on other fake news posts,** internet algorithms will present them with more fake stories, so their understanding of current events may be skewed.

" **"**
MAKE IT FUN FOR THEM TO FIND OUT MORE ABOUT THE POST.

HOW YOU COULD RESPOND

In the moment

Listen first
If you dismiss their view out of hand, they will become defensive, and their views more polarized and secretive. Assure them you are open to answering questions.

Be curious
Though it may be tempting to tell them not to be silly, start a conversation by asking questions. Offer to view the clip with them. You could say: "That's interesting. Who posted it? Do you know if this clip is from the original show or has it been changed to get more views?"

Encourage them to go on a detective hunt
Make it fun for them to find out more about the post. What else has the original account posted? Is the story also being covered by reputable websites? Could the clip have been "deep-faked"—edited to show events that never happened?

In the long term

Make them aware
Explain that fake news, scams, and ads are designed to trigger strong reactions so they get shared. Explain that those emotions are a clue to stop and think.

Give the bigger picture
Explain that hackers and conspiracy theorists work hard to make fake news look real and grown-ups can be fooled too. This sends the message that people of all ages need to ask questions because truth is important.

Explain facts versus opinions
Tell them that a fact is backed up by concrete evidence, which can be proven beyond doubt. An opinion is a personal view or judgment influenced by feelings.

Keep them connected
If your child is spending a lot of time alone online and is secretive, invite them to spend time with you. If they are trying out different views, keep talking about compromise, tolerance, and fact-checking.

"I DON'T NEED A **BABYSITTER**"

Now that your tween has mastered all the basic routines and can put themself to bed without your help, they may insist they no longer need a babysitter and relish the prospect of being home alone.

SCENARIO | When you tell your tween you are getting a babysitter, they insist they no longer need one.

As tweens get more independent, they may want to show they can survive without you. However, one of the trickiest tightropes parents will walk is deciding whether their child is ready for more freedom or whether they need more time to mature. Tweens don't consider themselves "little children" and look forward to adulthood, which means they can overestimate their capacities. However, if you don't allow them the opportunity to look after themselves, you may send the message that they are not capable of surviving without you, when independence is one of the main lessons of childhood.

> ### WHAT YOU MIGHT BE THINKING
> --------
> **You may agree your tween is responsible enough to be alone,** but wonder about their ability to cope if something goes wrong.

WHAT THEY MIGHT BE THINKING

- **Your tween may resent the rules of a babysitter** who doesn't know them well and who treats them in a more babyish way than you do.

- **They will argue their case logically,** as they believe they are old enough for their views to be considered.

- **Your tween may feel a mixture of excitement, responsibility,** and pride if they are being trusted when you leave the house, but may also be anxious to prove they can handle it.

- **If your tween is looking after younger siblings,** they may believe they are now the same level as a parent and be tempted to flex their power while you are out.

> ❝ ❞
> **PRACTICE LEAVING THEM AT HOME FOR SHORT PERIODS. KEEP IT BRIEF AT FIRST.**

HOW YOU COULD RESPOND

In the moment

Listen to their arguments
Give their request consideration. You can still say no, but your child's emotional and social development will benefit if you explain why.

Check your feelings
You may have a blind spot about letting your child have more independence. Keep your decisions grounded in what you know, rather than what you fear. If you find yourself saying no a lot, it may be time to review how much they are ready for. If parents are too anxious, children assume they are incapable and there must be a lot to worry about.

Do a responsibility inventory
Would they be mature enough to babysit for others? Have they shown good judgment? Do they do the things they are supposed to do each day, like brushing their teeth? Do they know how to lock and unlock the door and not to answer to strangers? If you don't feel they are ready, say it is a responsibility that you don't want them to have to bear yet.

Consider your neighborhood
Your decision will depend on more than your tween's maturity. Do you live in a high-crime area? Are there neighbors or family who can get to your house in an emergency?

In the long term

Give more responsibility
If your tween is not yet ready to be left home alone, give them opportunities to learn responsibility in other ways, such as planning a family outing or looking after pets.

Do trial runs
Practice leaving them at home for short periods. Keep it brief at first—about 30 minutes to an hour. When you get back, talk it

through. If all was well, you can increase the time you're away.

Prepare your home
Put measures in place: check smoke detectors and set parental controls on screens.

Give them practice
Role-play scenarios: what would they do if a stranger rang the bell or the fire alarm went off?

SEE RELATED TOPICS
Don't tell me what to do!: pp.118–119
I'll call you Dude, not Dad: pp.132–133

"I'M TURNING **VEGAN**"

Younger children tend to adopt their parents' beliefs without question. But now that your tween is developing the ability to think more critically, they may start developing their own ideas and ethics—and challenging yours.

SCENARIO | After seeing an online video posted by an animal rights group, your tween tells you they are turning vegan.

When they were younger, your child will have formed their views based on what they experienced and what you told them. Now that your tween is older and entering a new phase of cognitive development, they are starting to think in more abstract ways and are seeing the bigger picture. They are also looking for ways to experiment with new identities that are separate from you. For these reasons, your tween may be finding new causes to care about passionately, some of which may well be different from your own.

WHAT YOU MIGHT BE THINKING

You may be annoyed about any extra food preparation needed. You may also see it as a rejection, or even a criticism, of the diet you raised them on.

WHAT THEY MIGHT BE THINKING

⊚ **Your tween is experimenting with speaking their mind** and seeing what reaction they get, after having been told what to think as children. This can be exciting for them as well as scary.

⊚ **If you criticize their views without considering them**, your tween may feel you don't like the person they are becoming at a critical stage in their identity development. They may feel rejected and be likely to rebel.

⊚ **They may feel frustrated and more worried about the future**, and our ability to turn the climate crisis around, if you ridicule them. Going plant-based will help your tween feel like they can make a personal difference by reducing their carbon footprint and helping the environment.

⊚ **If your tween's diet is already disordered**, they may use a plant-based diet as an excuse to restrict what they eat.

HOW YOU COULD RESPOND

In the moment

Be curious
Rather than see your tween's decision as an affront to your values, find out their reasons. Treating their views with respect, even if you don't agree, will help build their self-worth and make them feel like they matter. It will also teach them to listen to other people's points of views.

See it as part of development
See your tween's views as a sign of healthy development and building their cognitive and interpersonal skills. Studies have found that adolescents who take part in activism go onto higher levels of education and higher incomes than those who don't.

Be vigilant
Check that they are not using it to hide disordered eating. Keep an eye on whether they are also exercising more, throwing away food, talking about their body shape, starting to hide their body, or going to the bathroom right after eating.

In the long term

Plan it together
Studies show that a nutritionally balanced plant-based diet is healthier for us and more sustainable for the planet. However, at this stage, your tween is likely to be drawn to less nutritious foods, such as processed snacks. Talk about the importance of a well-planned diet, with regular meals, so they get all the nutrients they need. Consider sourcing a multivitamin as a back-up. Show you care about the planet, too, and are willing to make more sustainable choices by preparing recipes together.

Keep communicating
Your tween will be asking more complex questions. Get used to the idea that though your opinion counts, they are now taking in information from many different sources. Be prepared to meet them in this new phase.

◀ **SEE RELATED TOPICS** ▶
You can't tell me what to eat!: pp.182–183
I'm doing a glow-up challenge: pp.196–197

❝ ❞

TREATING THEIR VIEWS WITH RESPECT WILL HELP BUILD THEIR SELF-WORTH.

"THEY ASKED ME FOR A NUDE PICTURE"

When your tween goes on social media, they are entering a world of billions of strangers. If you don't accompany them and set boundaries about where they wander, their inexperience can make them vulnerable.

SCENARIO | Your monitoring software flags up that your tween has been chatting to a stranger online who has asked them to send a nude photo.

So far, your child has been surrounded by grown-ups who have done all they can to keep them safe. So they won't yet understand the motives of a small but determined group of adults who want to take advantage of them. They have not yet developed the critical skills or confidence to question or say no to people older or more confident. As many as one in five young people will be sexually solicited by an adult stranger online in games, chat rooms, direct messages, and social media.

WHAT YOU MIGHT BE THINKING

You may panic when you realize your child has been approached by a potential abuser. You may feel guilty that you let your child have access to social media and did not put enough safety nets in place.

SEE RELATED TOPICS

My friend showed me this video on their phone: pp.158–159
It's online so it must be true: pp.188–189

WHAT THEY MIGHT BE THINKING

⊚ **Tweens tend to take what they are told at face value,** so they will not question it when their new "friend" has all the same hobbies and interests that they do.

⊚ **Tweens have been trained to be polite.** So they will find it hard to say no or tell someone they don't want to do something, especially if they seem kind and sympathetic and give them compliments.

⊚ **Older tweens are curious about how attractive they appear** to others. As they figure this out, they are more open to flattery, particularly if a predator pretends to be a peer who is a bit older.

⊚ **Your tween knows you view them as an "innocent" child** so may be too ashamed to tell you they have been having private conversations, which are now becoming uncomfortable.

TALK ABOUT HOW TO NOTICE WHEN THEY FEEL UNCOMFORTABLE.

HOW YOU COULD RESPOND

In the moment

Stay calm
Thank them for being brave and talking to you. When you are ready, ask what happened. Let them talk, and ask for a timeline. They need support, not criticism.

Reassure them
Tell them it's not the end of the world and that they won't get into trouble for making a mistake. The law exists to protect children, so they should not worry if you report it.

Take control quickly
Report the incident to site administrators using help or contact buttons. If you believe the picture was requested by a child at their school, contact the school, which should have staff trained to deal with it. If you believe it was an adult, report it to the police or a child protection agency.

Give context
Explain that there are some people online who bully others into doing things they don't want to do, and it can be hard to stand up to them without practice.

Explain this will pass
This can be a scary experience for a tween. By giving lots of comfort and reassurance, you can limit the damage.

In the long term

Educate them
Show your tween how to use neutral nicknames in their social media profiles—with no real pictures—so there are no clues to their age, gender, or address. Talk about how to notice when they feel uncomfortable about someone else's behavior and that it's always okay to say no or come to you and ask questions.

Stay connected
Online abusers pick victims who are lonely, unsupervised, naïve, and have low self-esteem. Showing you love spending time with your tween, and having a running conversation about their online lives, is the best protection.

Make them aware
Help them spot the signs of grooming. These include being asked to keep secrets, bringing up sexual topics, and being asked questions about who else uses their devices and where their parents are. Show your tween how to block and report, and forbid them from using screens alone in bedrooms or overnight.

"I'M DOING A **GLOW-UP** CHALLENGE"

Young people may copy influencers who put themselves through "self-improvement" challenges in a set amount of time to change their appearance. Stay connected to your tween so this goal doesn't take over their life.

SCENARIO | Your tween has started working out a lot, doing daily push-ups and jumping jacks, as part of an online glow-up challenge.

A "glow-up" has become a term used by young people for a noticeable transformation in looks, designed to make them more attractive to their peers. It's also used to describe a sudden transition from being awkward to more confident. However, while it's presented as "self-care," a glow-up can put pressure on young people to meet a conventionally "ideal" body type in an unrealistic time frame and meet other hard-to-achieve goals like "perfect" skin in as little as a month. Be there to support your tween in case their desire to change their appearance starts taking over their life.

WHAT YOU MIGHT BE THINKING

You may be pleased your tween is interested in exercising for good health but worried they are becoming too self-critical about how they look.

WHAT THEY MIGHT BE THINKING

⊚ **Your tween may think they aren't "good enough"** and that they don't fit in or get noticed. They feel they need to "improve."

⊚ **They may look up to the influencer** leading the challenge, not realizing that looking a certain way is their job and that they may use editing, lighting, and other digital tricks to enhance results.

⊚ **Glow-ups often come with time pressures** to achieve changes, which could lead your tween into overexercising, cutting back their calorie intake drastically, or purging to reach a target, like having a flat stomach. For some tweens, eating less and exercising more can become coping mechanisms for stress.

⊚ **Your tween may also start asking for skincare, makeup,** and beauty products to "fix" their perceived flaws if the glow-up challenge involves a full "makeover," then be disappointed when they don't experience the transformations they see online.

HOW YOU COULD RESPOND

In the moment

Be curious
Show an interest in the videos and ask them to talk you through the routines. Ask how they feel, rather than how much they are eating and exercising. You could say: "What do you feel you want to change?" Ask them about their goals and how they will know when they have reached them.

Give perspective
Girls gain up to 20 percent of their body weight during puberty.

If they are trying to lose weight to counter this, explain changing body shape is necessary as they develop into an adult.

Be vigilant
Your child will go through different phases, ranging from picky eating to constant snacking. Only a small number will develop an eating disorder, but be alert to the signs: hoarding food, eating alone, or expressing guilt about food or exercise.

In the long term

Stay connected
Spend time with your tween, doing activities together that have nothing to do with eating or exercising, whether it's watching a favorite TV show or doing a daily Wordle. Take a whole family approach to meals, too, eating together whenever possible and focusing on the conversation rather than on the food.

Keep listening
If they are exercising secretly, your tween may claim they are just

being "healthy." If you suggest they stop or cut back, they may worry you are taking away the coping mechanism that makes them feel in control. Keep talking and let your child know you are there when they are ready to talk.

Pressure on boys
Be aware that in recent years, the rate of disordered eating and exercise has increased among boys, partly in response to the rise in expectations about how males should look on social media.

SEE RELATED TOPICS
Am I fat?: pp.180–181
I'm turning vegan: pp.192–193

❝ ❞

SHOW AN INTEREST IN THE VIDEOS AND ASK THEM TO TALK YOU THROUGH THE ROUTINES.

BIBLIOGRAPHY

18–19 Don't do that, Mom!
Elkind, D. (1967). Egocentrism in adolescence. *Child Development*, Vol. 38, No. 4, pp.1025–1034

Somerville, L. H. (2013). Teens get more embarrassed by social evaluation. *Curr Dir Psychol Sci*, 2013 Apr 1; 22(2):121–127

20–21 Are we there yet?
Friedman, W. J., Janssen, S. M. J. (2010). Aging and the speed of time. *Acta Psychologica*, 134(2), pp.130–141

Knapton, S. (2022). Struggling with road trip tantrums? Here's how to buy 15 minutes of extra peace. *The Telegraph*. [online]

Lemlich, R. (1975). Subjective Acceleration of time with aging. *Perceptual and Motor Skills*, 41(1), pp.235–238

Ogden, R. (2022). "Are we nearly there yet?": Why long car journeys are so excruciating for your kids. The Conversation [online]

Reddan, M. C. et al (2018). Attenuating Neural Threat Expression with Imagination. *Neuron*

24–25 Communicating with tweens
Fair, D. et al (2008). The maturing architecture of the brain's default network. *Proceedings of the National Academy of Sciences*, 105(10), pp.4028-4032

Nencheva, M. L. et al (2023). Caregiver speech predicts the emergence of children's emotion vocabulary. *Child Development*, doi:https://doi.org/10.1111/cdev.13897

26–27 I want a dog
Bryant, B. K. (1990). The richness of the child-pet relationship: a consideration of benefits and costs of pets to children. *Anthrozoös*, 3(4), pp.253–261

Davis, J. H., Juhasz, A.M (1985). The preadolescent pet bond and psychological development. *Marriage and Family Review* 8

Melson, G. F. (2003). Child development and the human-companion animal bond. *American Behavioral Scientist*, 47(1), pp.31–39

Poresky, R. H., Others, A. (1988). Developmental benefits of pets for young children. *ERIC* [online]

28–29 Race you there
Pickhardt, C. (2022). Talking with adolescents about the importance of competition. *Psychology Today* [online]

32–33 Video gaming
NSPCC. www.nspcc.org.uk/keeping-children-safe/online-safety/online-games

Przybylski A. K. Weinstein N. (2016). How we see electronic games. PeerJ 4:e1931 https://doi.org/10.7717/peerj.1931

34–35 Is Santa real?
Anderson, C. J., Prentice, N. M. (1994). Encounter with reality: children's reactions on discovering the Santa Claus myth. *Child Psychiatry and Human Development*, 25(2), pp.67–84

Goldstein, T. R., Woolley, J. (2016). Ho! Ho! Who? Parent promotion of belief in and live encounters with Santa Claus. *Cognitive Development*, 39, pp.113–127

Shtulman, A., (2015). Children's understanding of physical possibility constrains their belief in Santa Claus. *Cognitive Development*, 34, pp.51–62

36–37 Just one more game
Children's Commissioner for England (2019). Gaming the system [online]

Przybylski, A. K., Weinstein, N. (2017). A large-scale test of the Goldilocks hyypothesis. *Psychological Science*, 28(2), pp.204–215

38–39 I'm a superhero!
Lamb, S. (2010). Today's superheroes send wrong image to boys. American Psychological Association [online]

Steinbeck, K. (2017). Health check: Do boys really have a testosterone spurt at age four? *The Conversation* [online]

Telford, R. M.et al. (2016) Why are girls less physically active than boys? *LOOK Longitudinal Study*' [online]

40–41 They're teasing me
Chen, Z. et al (2008). When hurt will not heal: exploring the capacity to relive social and physical pain. *Psychological Science* www.ncbi.nlm.nih.gov/ pubmed/18816286

Olweus, D. (1993). *Bullying at school: what we know and what we can do*. Wiley-Blackwell

42–43 I'm old enough to stay up late
GOSH. Sleep hygiene in children. www.gosh.nhs.uk/conditions-and-treatments/procedures-and-treatments/sleep-hygiene-children

44–45 I want a hug
Ardiel E., Rankin C. (2010). The importance of touch in development. *Paediatr Child Health*. 15(3):153-156

Aznar, A., Tenenbaum, H. R. (2016). Parent–child positive touch: gender, age, and task differences. *Journal of Nonverbal Behavior*, 40(4), pp.317–333

Brauer, J. et al (2016). Frequency of maternal touch predicts resting activity and connectivity of the developing social brain. *Cerebral Cortex*, 26, 3544-3552

Buchheim A., et al (2009). Oxytocin enhances the experience of attachment security. *Psychoneuroendocrinology* [online]

Narvaez, D. et al (2019). The importance of early life touch for psychosocial and moral development. *Psicologia: Reflexão e Crítica*, 32(1).

Stokes, P. E. (1995). The potential role of excessive cortisol induced by HPA hyperfunction in the pathogenesis of depression. *European Neuropsychopharmacology* [online]

46–47 Nothing's the matter
Reddan M. C. et al (2018). Attenuating neural threat expression with imagination. *Neuron*, 100 (4): 994

48–49 Keep out!
American Academy of Child & Adolescent Psychiatry (2017). *Adolescent development: part 1* [online]

Arain M. et al (2013). Maturation of the adolescent brain. *Neuropsychiatr Dis Treat.* 2013;9:449-61

Hawk, S. T. (2017). Chinese adolescents' reports of covert parental monitoring: Comparisons with overt monitoring and links with information management. *Journal of Adolescence*, Vol. 55

Oudekerk B. A. et al (2015). The cascading development of autonomy and relatedness from adolescence to adulthood. *Child Dev.* 2015;86(2):472-85

50–51 Pocket money
Bucciol, A., Veronesi, M. (2013). Teaching children to save and lifetime savings: what is the best strategy? *Journal of Economic Psychology* 45 (2013), pp1–17

Furnham, A. F. (2001). Parental attitudes towards pocket money/allowances for children. *Journal of Economic Psychology*, 22 pp397–422

Furnham, A. (1999). The saving and spending habits of young people. *Journal of Forensic Psychology* 20, pp.677–697

Rubin, R. (2004). Kids vs. teens: money and maturity guide to online behaviour," *eMarket* [online]

Strauss, A., Schuessler, K. (1951). Socialization, logical reasoning and concept development in the child. *American Sociological Review* 16, pp.514–523

Webley, P. et al (1993). A study in economic psychology: Children's saving in a play economy. *Economics and Psychology*, pp.61–80

56–57 I was only joking!
Psych Central (2016). How children develop empathy. https://psychcentral.com/lib/how-children-develop-empathy#1

Psych Central (2016). Humor as a key to child development [online]

Sciencedirect.com (2019). The psychology of humor. www.sciencedirect.com/book/9780123725646/the-psychology-of-humor

Wiseman, R. (2014). *Masterminds & Wingmen: Helping our boys cope with schoolyard power, locker-room tests, girlfriends, and the new rules of boy world*, Harmony

58–59 They say I'm a show-off
Brummelman, E., Sander, T. (2017). How children construct views of themselves: a social-developmental perspective. *Child Development*, [online]

Brummelman, E. et al (2015). Origins of narcissism in children. PNAS [online]

60–61 I've got nothing to do
Faber, A., Mazlish, E. (2006). *How to talk so teens will listen and listen so teens will talk*, Piccadilly

Mann, S., Cadman, R. (2014). Does being bored make us more creative? *Creativity Research Journal* 26, no. 2, pp.165–173

Martz, M. E. et al (2016) "I am so bored!": prevalence rates and sociodemographic and contextual correlates of high boredom among American adolescents. *Youth & Society* 50, no. 5 pp.688–710

Pellegrini, A. D., Bohn-Gettler, C. M. (2013). The benefits of recess in primary school. *Scholarpedia* 8, no. 2, p30448

Rhodes, E. (2015). The exciting side of boredom. *The Psychologist* 28, no. 4, pp278–281

Singer, D. G. et al (2009). Children's pastimes and play in sixteen nations: is free-play declining? *American Journal of Play* 1, no. 3, pp.283–312

Wahlstrom, D. et al (2010) Developmental changes in dopamine neurotransmission in adolescence: behavioral implications and issues in assessment. *Brain and Cognition 72*, no. 1 (2010), pp146–159

62–63 All my friends have a phone
Collier, K. M. et al (2016). Does parental mediation of media influence child outcomes? A meta-analysis on media time, aggression, substance use, and sexual behavior. *Developmental Psychology* 52, no. 5, pp.798–812

Livingstone, S. et al (2017). Children's online activities, risks and safety: a literature review by the UKCCIS Evidence Group. UK Council for Child Internet Safety

64–65 Climate change
Clayton, S., Manning, C. (2018). *Psychology and climate change: human perceptions, impacts, and responses*, Academic Press

Mind. Time in Nature improves mental well-being. www.mind.org.uk/information-support/tips-for-everyday-living/nature-and-mental-health/

Ojala, M. (2017). Young People and Climate Change Communication, www.researchgate.net/publication/314672232_Young_People_and_Climate_Change_Communication

The Climate Outreach and Information Network. How do young people engage with climate change? https://climateaccess.org/system/files/COIN_Young%20Voices.pdf

68–69 I just can't sit still
Cross, J. What does too much screen time do to children's brains? Health Matters [online]

Madigan, S. (2019). Association between screen time and children's performance on a developmental screening test. JAMA Pediatrics. [online]

Radesky, J. S. (2015). Mobile and interactive media use by young children: the good, the bad, and the unknown. *Pediatrics*. DOI: https://doi.org/10.1542/peds.2014-2251

Santos, R.M.S. et al (2022). The association between screen time and attention in children: a systematic review. *Developmental Neuropsychology*, 47(4), pp.1–18

Vaidyanathan, S. et al (2020). Screen time exposure in preschool children with ADHD: a cross-sectional exploratory study from South India. *Indian Journal of Psychological Medicine*, p.025371762093978

72–73 They didn't save me a seat at lunchtime
Simmons, R. (2011). *Odd girl out: the hidden culture of aggression in girls*, Mariner Books

Simmons, R. (2010). *The curse of the good girl: raising authentic girls with courage and confidence*, Penguin

Wiseman, R. (2003). *Queen bees and wannabes: helping your daughter survive cliques, gossip, boyfriends and the realities of girl world*, Piatkus

76–77 We were just pretending
Arnott, G. (2020). Play fighting helps equip animals for later life—new research. *The Conversation* [online]

Pellegrini A.D (1995). A longitudinal study of boys' rough-and-tumble play and dominance during early adolescence. *J Appl Dev Psychol*;16:77–93

Pellegrini, A. D. (1994). The rough play of adolescent boys of differing sociometric status. *Int J Behav Dev*.;17:525–540

Ross, H., Taylor, H. (1989) Do boys prefer daddy or his physical style of play? *Sex Roles*; 20:23–33

Smith, P. K. (2010). *Children and play*, Wiley-Blackwell

78–79 Are you going to die too?
Child Bereavement UK. www.childbereavementuk.org/information-childrens-understanding-of-death

Hopkins, M. (2014). The development of children's understanding of death. University of East Anglia [online]

80–81 It's not gross; it's funny!
Carson, D. K. et al (1986). Temperament and communicative competence as predictors of young children's humor. *Merrill-Palmer Quarterly*, Vol. 32, No. 4, pp.415-426

Chapman, A. J. (1979). Social aspects of humourous laughter. *Przeglad Psychologiczn*, Vol. 22, No. 1, pp.89-124

Dews, S. et al. (1996). Children's understanding of the meaning and functions of verbal irony. *Child Development*, Vol. 67, No. 6, pp.3071-3085

Lyon, C. (2006). Humour and the young child: a review of the research literature [online]

Rottman, J. (2014). Evolution, development, and the emergence of disgust. *Evolutionary Psychology*, 12(2), p.147470491401200

82–83 Can I go on a sleepover?
Gittens, G. (2017). Children as young as nine exposed to porn on sleepovers. Independent.ie [online]

84–85 Sibling relationships
Kowal, A., Kramer, L. (2006). Children's understanding of parental differential treatment. *Child Development* 68, no. 1

86–87 I want a makeover party
Topping, A. (2018). *Girls as young as 7 feel pressure to be pretty—body confidence study.* The Guardian [online]

www.mintel.com (2012). *Beauty basics targeting younger faces.* Mintel [online]

88–89 I got the best grade
Curran, T., Hill, A. (2019). Perfectionism Is increasing over time: a meta-analysis of birth cohort differences from 1989 to 2016. *Psychological Bulletin,* www.apa.org/pubs/journals/releases/bul-bul0000138.pdf

Pickhardt C. (2013). *Surviving your child's adolescence,* Wiley

92–93 I'm a loser
Chansky, T. (2008). *Freeing your child from negative thinking,* Da Capo books

Cherry, K. (2022). Industry vs. inferiority in psychosocial development. Verywell Mind. [online]

Marenus, M. (2020). Gardner's theory of multiple intelligences. Simply Psychology [online]

Wheeler, L. (1966). Motivation as a determinant of upward comparison. *J. Exp. Soc. Psychol.* 1, pp.27–31

96–97 I don't want to go to Grandma's
Moorman, S. M., and Stokes, J. E. (2014). Solidarity in the grandparent–adult grandchild relationship and trajectories of depressive symptoms. *The Gerontologist,* 56(3), pp.408–420

98–99 That's babyish
Klemenovic, J. (2014). How do today's children play and with which toys? *Croatian Journal of Education,* 16. pp.181-200

Morris, S. (2007). *Why children become so attached to toys and comfort blankets.* The Guardian [online]

100–101 Separation and divorce
Baxter, L. A. et al (1999). Turning points in the development of blended family relationships. *Journal of Social and Personal Relationships,* 16(3), pp291-313

Bernstein, E. (2016). How long does it take to unite a stepfamily? *The Wall Street Journal* [online]

Portrie, T., Hill, N. (2005). Blended families: a critical review of the current research. *The Family Journal* [online]

102–103 I need a bra
Benedek, E. P. et al (1979). A note on the female adolescent's psychological reactions to breast development. *Journal of the American Academy of Child and Adolescent Psychiatry* 18, pp.537–545

Brooks-Gunn, J. et al (1994). The experience of breast development and girls' stories about the purchase of a bra. *Journal of Youth and Adolescence* 23, no. 5, pp.539–565

Scurr, J. et al (2016). The influence of the breast on sport and exercise participation in school girls in the United Kingdom. *Journal of Adolescent Health* 58, no. 2, pp.167–173

Wolters Kluwer Health (2014). Study shows mental health impact of breast size differences in teens. *Science Daily* [online]

104–105 I'm not pretty enough
Hogue, J. V., Mills, J. S. (2019). The effects of active social media engagement with peers on body image in young women. *Body Image* 28, pp.1–5

Jones, D. C. (2001). Social comparison and body image: Attractiveness comparisons to models and peers among adolescent girls and boys. *Sex Roles;* 45:pp.645–664

Jovanovic, J. et al (1989). Objective and subjective attractiveness and early adolescent adjustment. *Journal of Adolescence;*12:pp.225–229

108–109 I don't want to go to school
Blagg, N. (1987). *School phobia and its Treatment,* Routledge

Elliott, J., Place, M. (2004). *Children in difficulty: a guide to understanding and helping,* Routledge

Fremont, W. P. (2003). School refusal in children and adolescents. *American Family Physician* 68, no. 8, pp.1555–1561

Ingles, C. J. et al (2015). Current status of research on school refusal. *European Journal of Education and Psychology* 8, no. 1, pp.37–52

Williams, E. (2004). The issue: school phobia. *The Times Educational Supplement* [online]

Wimmer, M. (2010). School refusal: information for educators. *Helping Children at Home and School III,* National Association of School Psychologists [online]

110–111 I'm going to be famous when I grow up
Min, S. (2019). 86% of young Americans want to become a social media influencer. CBS News [online]

Papadatou, A. (2019). 1 of 5 British children want a career as social media influencers. *HR Review* [online]

Willment, N. (2022). "Influencer" is now a popular career choice for young people—here's what you should know about the creator economy's dark side. *The Conversation* [online]

112–113 Puberty
Cesario, S. K.,Hughes, L. A. (2007). Precocious puberty: a comprehensive review of literature. *Journal of Obstetric, Gynecologic & Neonatal Nursing,* 36(3), pp.263–274

Eckert-Lind, C. et al (2020). Worldwide secular trends in age at pubertal onset assessed by breast development among girls: a systematic review and meta-analysis. jamanetwork.com/journals/jamapediatrics/fullarticle/2760573

114–115 They posted a mean message
Atherton, O. E. et al, (2017). Bidirectional pathways between relational aggression and temperament from late childhood to adolescence. *J Res Pers.;* 67:75-84

Blakely-McClure, S. J., Ostrov, J. M. (2016). Relational aggression, victimization and self-concept: testing pathways from middle childhood to adolescence. *J Youth Adolesc.;* 45(2):376-90. doi:10.1007/s10964-015-0357-2

Patchin, J. W., Hinduja, S. (2021). Cyberbullying among tweens in the United States: prevalence, impact, and helping behaviors. *The Journal of Early Adolescence,* 42(3), p.027243162110367

Simmons, R. (2011). *Odd girl out: the hidden culture of aggression in girls,* Mariner Books

120–121 Starting middle school
Pascoe, M. C., et al (2020). The impact of stress on students in secondary school and higher education. *International Journal of Adolescence and Youth* 25(1), pp.104–112

124–125 Why can't I go on TikTok?
Bennett, M., Bennett, S. (2019) How to talk to kids about social media and respect. Brightly. www.readbrightly.com/how-to-talk-to-kids-about-social-media-and-self-respect/

Common Sense Media (2018). Social media, social life: teens reveal their experiences [online]

Gold, J. (2015). *Screen smart parenting: how to find balance and benefit in your child's use of social media, apps and digital devices.,* The Guilford Press, New York

Kidron, Baroness B. (with Rudkin, Dr. A.) (2017). Digital childhood: addressing childhood development milestones in the digital environment. www.researchgate.net/publication/322505114_Digital_Childhood_Addressing_childhood_development_milestones_in_the_digital_environment

Lacey, B. (2007). Social aggression: a study of internet harassment. Hofstra University. www.

learntechlib.org/p/123761/ Ofcom report (2022): www.ofcom.org.uk/__data/assets/pdf_file/0024/234609/childrens-media-use-and-attitudes-report-2022.pdf

Twenge, J. (2017). *iGen: why today's super-connected kids are growing up less rebellious, more tolerant, less happy—and completely unprepared for adulthood*, Atria, New York

126–127 I can fast-forward the bad parts
Coker, T. R. et al (2015). Media violence exposure and physical aggression in fifth-grade children. *Acad Pediatr.*;15(1):pp.82–88

Gentile, D. A. et al (2014). Protective effects of parental monitoring of children's media use: a prospective study. *JAMA Pediatr.*;168(5):479-484. doi:10.1001/jamapediatrics.2014.146

128–129 I am so going to marry them
Pickhardt, C. (2012) Adolescence and the teenage crush. *Psychology Today* [online]

130–131 Body image
Alleva, J. M. et al (2021). I appreciate your body, because… does promoting positive body image to a friend affect one's own positive body image? *Body Image*, 36

Bassett-Gunter, R. et al (2017). Physical activity and body image among men and boys: a meta-analysis. *Body Image*, 22(1):pp.114–28

Campbell, A., Hausenblas, H. A. (2009). Effects of exercise interventions on body image: a meta-analysis. *J Health Psychol.* Sep 17;14(6):pp.780–93

Dunaev, J. et al (2018). An attitude of gratitude: the effects of body-focused gratitude on weight bias internalization and body image. *Body Image*, 25, pp.9–13

Krayer, A. et al (2008) Social comparison and body image in adolescence: a grounded theory approach. *Health Education Research* 23, no. 5, pp.892–903

Mental Health Foundation (2019). Body image report—executive summary. [online] www.mentalhealth.org.uk/explore-mental-health/articles/body-image-report-executive-summary

Mental Health Foundation (2022). How can we protect, promote, and maintain body image? [online] www.mentalhealth.org.uk/our-work/research/body-image-how-we-think-and-feel-about-our-bodies/how-can-we-protect-promote-and-maintain-body-image

Russell-Mayhew, S. (2014). Puberty and body image. *Eating Disorders Resource Cat.* [online]

SantaBarbara, N. J. et al (2017). A systematic review of the effects of resistance training on body image. *Journal of Strength and Conditioning Research*;31(1):2880–8

Wertheim, E. H., Paxton, S. J. (2012). Body image development: adolescent girls. *Encyclopedia of body image and human appearance*, pp.187-193)

132–133 I'll call you Dude, not Dad
Pickhardt, C. (2010). The challenge of mothering an adolescent son. *Psychology Today* [online]

134–135 I'm getting spots
Gieler, U. et al (2015) Acne and quality of life—impact and management." *J Eur Acad Dermatol Venereol*;29 Suppl 4:12-4

Revol, O. et al (2015). Psychological impact of acne on 21st-century adolescents: decoding for better care. *Br J Dermatol.*;172 Suppl 1:52-8

Zaenglein, A. L. (2010). Making the case for early treatment of acne. *Clin Pediatr.*; 49(1):54-9

136–137 Anxiety
Anwar, Y. (2013). Sleep deprivation boosts anticipatory anxiety. *Science Daily* [online]

Code, D. (2011). Stressed parents create stressed kids—kids pick up on everything: how parental stress is toxic to kids, Createspace

Ehmke, R. (2016). Anxiety in the classroom. Child Mind Institute [online]

Grimm, S. et al (2014). Early life stress modulates oxytocin effects on limbic system during acute psychosocial stress. *Social Cognitive and Affective Neuroscience*, 9(11), pp.1828–1835

Hurrell, K. E. et al (2017). Parental meta-emotion philosophy and emotion coaching in families of children and adolescents with an anxiety disorder. *Journal of Abnormal Child Psychology* 45, no. 3, pp.569–582

Hostinar, C. E., Gunnar, M. R. (2015). Social support can buffer against stress and shape brain activity. *AJOB Neuroscience* 6, no 3, pp34–42

Leiner, M., et al (2016). Mental and emotional health of children exposed to news media of threats and acts of terrorism: the cumulative and pervasive effects. *Frontiers in Pediatrics*, [online]

NHS Inform. Anxiety disorders in children. www.nhsinform.scot/illnesses-and-conditions/mental-health/anxiety-disorders-in-children#:~:text=not%20eating%20properly

Sunderland, M., Armstrong, N. (2001). *Helping children who are anxious or obsessional: a guidebook*, Routledge

138–139 I'm scared I won't get a good grade
Curran, T. (2017). Perfectionism is increasing over time: a meta-analysis of birth cohort differences from 1989 to 2016. APA [online]

Levine, M. (2013). *Teach your children well: why values and coping skills matter more than grades, trophies, or "fat envelopes,"* Harper Perennial

Levine, M. (2008). *The price of privilege: how parental pressure and material advantage are creating a generation of disconnected and unhappy kids*, Harper Paperbacks

Pickhardt, C. (2013). *Surviving your child's adolescence*, Wiley

140–141: My selfie got 100 likes!
Bell, B. T. (2019). You take fifty photos, delete forty nine and use one: a qualitative study of adolescent image-sharing practices on social media. *International Journal of Child-Computer Interaction*,Vol. 20, pp.64-71, ISSN 2212-8689

Lamp, S. et al (2019). Picture perfect: the relationship between selfie behaviors, self-objectification, and depressive symptoms. *Sex Roles* 81(11–12)

Mental Health Foundation (2019). Body image report—executive summary. [online] www.mentalhealth.org.uk/explore-mental-health/articles/body-image-report-executive-summary

ScienceDaily (2011). Accentuating the positive may eliminate the negative in teenagers with anxiety. www.sciencedaily.com/releases/2011/07/110712190557.htm.

144–145 Pornography
Children's Commissioner for England (2023). "A lot of it is actually just abuse"—young people and pornography [online]

Doornwaard, S. et al (2017). Dutch adolescents' motives, perceptions and reflections towards sex-related internet use: results of a web-based focus-group study. *Journal of Sex Research* 54, 8

Kyriaki, A. et al (2018). Adolescent pornography use: a systematic literature review of research trends 2000–2017. *Current Psychiatry Review* 14, no. 1

Love, T. et al (2015). Neuroscience of internet pornography addiction: a review and update. *Behavioural Sciences (Basel)* 5, no. 3, pp388–433

Martellozzo, E. et al (2016). "I wasn't sure it was normal to watch it": a quantitative and qualitative examination of the impact of online pornography on the values, attitudes, beliefs and behaviours of children and young people. Middlesex University [online]

Voon, V. et al (2014). Neural correlates of sexual cue reactivity in individuals with and without compulsive sexual Behaviours. *PLoS One* [online]

For free resources to help you talk to your child about porn, go to Culture Reframed: www.culturereframed.org/parents-program

146–147 My teacher hates me!
Suldo, S. et al (2009). Teacher support and adolescents' subjective well-being. *School Psychology Review* 38, no. 1, pp.67–85.

148–149 When will I get my period?
Koff, E., Rierdan, J. (1995). Preparing girls for menstruation. APA PsycNet [online]

Lacroix, A. E. et al (2019). Physiology, Menarche. National Library of Medicine [online]

Marques, P. et al (2022). Menstrual cycle among adolescents: girls' awareness and influence of age at menarche and overweight. National Library of Medicine [online]

152–153 They tease me about my boobs
Graber, J. A. (2013). Pubertal timing and the development of psychopathology in adolescence and beyond. *Hormones and Behavior*, 64, 262–269

Greenspan, L., Deardorff, J. (2014). *The new puberty: how to navigate early development in today's girls*, Rodale, New York

154–155 What's happening to my voice?
Harries, M. et al (1998). Changes in the male voice at puberty: vocal fold length and its relationship to the fundamental frequency of the voice. *J Laryngol Otol.*;112(5):451-4

156–157 She's a slut
Goblet, M., Glowacz, F. (2021). Slut shaming in adolescence: a violence against girls and its impact on their health. *International Journal of Environmental Research and Public Health*, [online] 18(12), p.6657

Ofsted (2021). Culture change needed to tackle "normalized" sexual harassment in schools and colleges. Gov.uk [online]

Wesche, R. et al (2019). Peer acceptance and sexual behaviors from adolescence to young adulthood. *Journal of Youth and Adolescence*, Vol 48(5), May 1, pp.996-1008

Wiseman, R. (2009). *Queen bees & wannabes: helping your daughter survive cliques, bossip, boyfriends, and the new realities of girl world*, Harmony Books

160–161 I'm so tired
Baum, K. T. et al (2013). Sleep restriction worsens mood and emotion regulation in adolescents. *Journal of Child Psychology and Psychiatry*, [online] 55(2), pp.180–190

Hale, L. et al (2018). Youth screen media habits and sleep. *Child and Adolescent Psychiatric Clinics of North America*, 27(2), pp.229–245

Scott, H. et al (2019). Social media use and adolescent sleep patterns. *BMJ Open*, 9(9), pp.1–9

162–163 I dare you!
Chick, C. F. (2015). Reward processing in the adolescent brain: individual differences and relation to risk taking. *The Journal of Neuroscience*, 35(40), pp.13539–13541

164–165 Gender
NSPCC. (2021). Gender identity. [online] www.nspcc.org.uk/keeping-children-safe/sex-relationships/gender-identity/

YoungMinds. Gender Identity & Mental Health: Guide For Parents.www.youngminds.org.uk/parent/parents-a-z-mental-health-guide/gender-identity/

166–167 I am telling the truth
Debey, E. et al (2015). From junior to senior Pinocchio: a cross-sectional lifespan investigation of deception. *Acta Psychologica* 160, pp.58–68

Engels, M. et al (2006). Lying behavior, family functioning and adjustment in early adolescence. *Journal of Youth and Adolescence* 35, no. 6, pp.949–958

Lavoie, J. et al (2017) Developmental profiles of children's spontaneous lie-telling behavior. *Cognitive Development* 41, (2017), pp33–45

Smith, J. A. (2017). What's good about lying? *Greater Good Magazine* [online]

168–169 Can I have a sip?
Clark, D. B. et al (2008). Alcohol, psychological dysregulation, and adolescent brain development. *Alcoholism: Clinical and Experimental Research* 32, no. 3, pp.375–384

Drinkaware. Talking to your child about alcohol, www.drinkaware.co.uk/advice/underage-drinking/talking-to-your-child-about-alcohol

Ellickson, P. L. et al (2003). Ten-year prospective study of public health problems associated with early drinking. *Pediatrics* 11, no. 5, pp.949–955

Nagel, B. J. et al (2005). Reduced hippocampal volume among adolescents with alcohol use disorders without psychiatric comorbidity. *Psychiatry Research*, 139, no. 3, pp181–190

Newbury-Birch, D. et al (2009). Impact of alcohol consumption on young people: a systematic review of published reviews. *Department for Children, Schools and Families*, Research Report DCSF-RR067

Sindelar, H. A. et al (2004). Adolescent alcohol use and injury: a summary and critical review of the literature. *Minerva pediatrica* 56, no. 3, pp.291–309

Tael-Öeren, M. et al (2019). The relationship between parental attitudes and children's alcohol use: a systematic review and meta-analysis. *Addiction* 114, no.9

170–171 How tall will I get?
Bisi, M. C., R. Stagni (2016). Development of gait motor control: what happens after a sudden increase in height during adolescence? *BioMedical Engineering Online* 15, no. 47

Oldehinkel, A. J. et al (2007). Being admired or being liked: classroom social status and depressive problems in early adolescent girls and boys. *J Abnorm Child Psychol* 35, no. 3, pp.417–427

Pattiselanno, K. et al (2015). Structure matters: the role of clique hierarchy in the relationship between adolescent social status and aggression and prosociality. *Journal of Youth and Adolescence* 44, no. 12, pp.2257–2274

Rogol, A. D. et al (2000). Growth and pubertal development in children and adolescents: effects of diet and physical activity. *The American Journal of Clinical Nutrition* 72, no. 2

Stanford Medicine Children's Health. The growing child: teenager (13 to 18 Years). www.stanfordchildrens.org/en/topic/default?id=the-growing-child-adolescent-13-to-18-years-90-P02175

Wiseman, R. (2003). *Ringleaders & sidekicks: how to help your son cope with classroom politics, bullying, girls and growing Up*, Piatkus

172–173 I need new sneakers
Brown, J. A. (2001). Media literacy and critical television viewing in education. *Handbook of Children and the Media*, Thousand Oaks, CA: Sage;681–697

Hudders, L. et al (2017). Shedding new light on how advertising literacy can affect children's processing of embedded advertising formats: A future research agenda. *Journal of Advertising*, 46(2), 333-349

McCannon, B. (2002). Media literacy: What? Why? How? *Children, Adolescents, and the Media*, Thousand Oaks, CA: Sage;322–367

Richins, M. L., Chaplin, L. N. (2015). Material parenting: how the use of goods in parenting fosters materialism in the next generation. *Journal of Consumer Research*;41(6),1333–1357

174–175 They're just scratches
Jones, A. C. et al (2011). Changes in loneliness during middle childhood predict risk for adolescent suicidality indirectly through mental health problems. *Journal of Clinical Child & Adolescent Psychology*, 40(6), pp.818–824

Paul, E., Ortin, A. (2019). Psychopathological mechanisms of early neglect and abuse on suicidal ideation and self-harm in middle childhood. *European Child & Adolescent Psychiatry*

176–177 I didn't mean to punch the wall
Byrne, M. L. et al (2017). A systematic review of adrenarche as a sensitive period in neurobiological development and mental health.*Developmental Cognitive Neuroscience*,Vol.25

178–179 The digital world
OECD. Children and young people's mental health in the digital age: shaping the future: www.oecd.org/els/health-systems/Children-and-Young-People-Mental-Health-in-the-Digital-Age.pdf

Twenge, J. (2017). *iGen: why today's super-connected kids are growing up less rebellious, more tolerant, less happy—and completely unprepared for adulthood*, Atria, New York

180–181 Am I fat?
Jones, M. D. et al (2014). A naturalistic study of fat talk and its behavioral and affective consequences. *Body Image*, 11(4), pp.337–345.

Robinson, B. E. (2020). The 90-second rule that builds self-control. *Psychology Today* [online]

Sole-Smith, V. (2023). *Fat talk: coming of age in diet culture*, Ithaka

182–183 You can't tell me what to eat!
Berge, J. M. et al (2013). Parent conversations about healthful eating and weight. JAMA Pediatrics, 167(8), p.746

Harrison, M. E. et al (2015). Systematic review of the effects of family meal frequency on psychosocial outcomes in youth. *Canadian Family Physician* 61(2), pp.e96–e106

184–185 Why can't I wear mascara to school?
Bradshaw, H. K, DelPriore D. J. (2021). Beautification is more than mere mate attraction. *Archives of Sexual Behavior*, 10.1007/s10508-021-01952-7, 51, 1, (43-47)

Critchell, S. (2010). Girls' interest in makeup fades with age.Today. www.today.com/news/girls-interest-makeup-fades-age-wbna3856621

Mintel (2016). Beauty is child's play: 80% of US tweens use beauty and personal care products. www.mintel.com/press-centre/beauty-is-childs-play-80-of-us-tweens-use-beauty-and-personal-care-products/

186–187 It's not my job
Brand, A. (2023). British parents are forced to work longer hours. [online] HR Review [online]

Hill, A. (2009). Lack of household chores making children less responsible, claims survey. *The Guardian* [online]

Li, S. (2016). "It's all about me, me, me!" Why children are spending less time doing household chores. The Conversation

Rossman, M. (2014). Involving children in household tasks. Is it worth the effort, University of Minnesota

Rutherford, M. B. (2009). Children's autonomy and responsibility: an analysis of childrearing advice. Qualitative Sociology, 32(4), pp.337–353

188–189 It's online so it must be true
Synak, N. et al (2022). Correlations among high school students' beliefs about conspiracy, authoritarianism, and scientific literacy. *Science & Education* [online]

Wallace, K. (2017). Is "fake news" fooling kids? New report says yes. CNN [online]

192–193 I'm turning vegan
BDA (2017). British Dietetic Association confirms well-planned vegan diets can support healthy living in people of all ages. BDA [online]

Darling, N. et al (2006). Predictors of adolescents' disclosure to parents and perceived parental knowledge: between- and within-person differences. *Journal of Youth and Adolescence* 35, no. 4, pp659–670

Maker Castro, E. M. et al (2022) Critical consciousness and well-being in adolescents and young adults: a systematic review. *Adolesc. Res. Rev.*, 7, 499–522

194–195 They asked me for a nude picture
Greene-Colozzi, E. A., et al (2020). Experiences and perceptions of online sexual solicitation and grooming of minors: a retrospective report. *Journal of Child Sexual Abuse*, 29(7), pp.836–854

Internet Matters. What steps can I take if my child has sent a nude? www.internetmatters.org/hub/question/steps-can-i-take-child-sent-nude/#:~:text=It

Milmo, D. (2022). 2021 was worst year on record for online child sexual abuse, says IWF. [online] The Guardian [online]

Quayle, Dr. E. (2017). Over the internet, under the radar: online child sexual abuse and exploitation—a brief literature review. Children and Young People's Centre for Justice [online]

INDEX

THE AUTHOR

Tanith Carey is a parenting writer and award-winning journalist. She is the author of 11 parenting and psychology books, which analyze some of the most urgent issues for today's parents and offer practical, research-based solutions. Tanith's books have been translated into 35 languages, including Spanish, French, Italian, German, and Chinese and have received widespread global media coverage. Her books include *What's My Child Thinking?* (DK), *What's My Teenager Thinking?* (DK), *The Friendship Maze* (Vie), *Taming the Tiger Parent* (Robinson), and *Girls Uninterrupted: Steps for building stronger girls in a challenging world* (Icon Books). Tanith's speaking engagements have included the Child Mind Institute in Palo Alto, California, and The Cheltenham Science Festival, UK. She has two children and holds a Certificate in Therapeutic Skills and Studies from London's Metanoia Institute, where she is training in Gestalt psychotherapy. For a full biography, see www.tanithcarey.com.

THE CONSULTANT

Dr. Angharad Rudkin is a Clinical Psychologist and Associate Fellow of the British Psychological Society. She has worked with children, adolescents, and families for more than 20 years and also lectured at the University of Southampton for 12 years. Angharad has an independent therapy practice and consults on child mental health to a number of organizations and systems. She has co-authored six books for children and parents and is a relationship expert for London's *Metro* daily newspaper. Angharad appears on TV and radio regularly as an expert on child and family issues.

ACKNOWLEDGMENTS

From the Author Thanks to my children, Lily and Clio, who have always been my inspiration. Also love to my husband, Anthony, whose support has allowed me to take the time to write these books. As always the process of writing the book has been made so much easier by working with Dr. Angharad Rudkin and her warm, solution-focused approach to everything that parenting brings up.

From the Consultant Thank you to all the researchers whose findings give us essential insight into our tweens, and a great big thank you to Tanith for putting these findings together in such a clear way, with patience, efficiency, and compassion. Thanks to the DK team; it has been lovely to work with you all again. I am indebted to the families I work with and who I constantly learn from. Finally, thank you, as always, to my wonderful family.

From the Publisher We would like to thank Dawn Bates for the copy edit, Emma and Tom Forge for their design work, Dr. Carl Pickhardt for consulting on the US edition, Jodie Gaudet for the proofread, and Hilary Bird for the index.

Penguin
Random
House

Senior Acquisitions Editor Becky Alexander
Senior Editor Sophie Blackman
US Senior Editor Jennette ElNaggar
Senior Designer Glenda Fisher
Senior Production Editor Tony Phipps
Senior Production Controller Stephanie McConnell
Jacket Designer Eleanor Ridsdale
Jacket and Sales Materials Co-ordinator Emily Cannings
Editorial Manager Ruth O'Rourke
Art Director Maxine Pedliham
Publishing Director Katie Cowan

Editorial Dawn Bates
Design Emma Forge, Tom Forge
Illustration Céleste Wallaert

First American Edition, 2024
Published in the United States by DK Publishing
1745 Broadway, 20th Floor, New York, NY 10019

Text copyright © Tanith Carey 2024

Copyright © 2024 Dorling Kindersley Limited
DK, a Division of Penguin Random House LLC
24 25 26 27 28 10 9 8 7 6 5 4 3 2 1
001–338947–Jan/2024

A catalog record for this book is available
from the Library of Congress.
ISBN 978-0-7440-9227-1

Printed and bound in China

www.dk.com

MIX
Paper | Supporting
responsible forestry
FSC™ C018179

This book was made with Forest
Stewardship Council™ certified
paper—one small step in DK's
commitment to a sustainable future.
**For more information go to
www.dk.com/our-green-pledge**

Disclaimer
The information in this book has been compiled as general
guidance on the specific subjects addressed. It is not a
substitute and not to be relied on for medical, healthcare, or
pharmaceutical professional advice. If you have any concerns
about any aspect of your child's behavior, health, or well-being,
please seek professional advice. Seek medical advice
before changing, stopping, or starting any of your child's
medical treatment. So far as the author is aware, the
information given is correct and up to date as of August 2023.
Practice, laws, and regulations all change, and the reader
should obtain up-to-date professional advice on any such
issues. The author and publishers disclaim, as far as the law
allows, any liability arising directly or indirectly from the use or
misuse of the information contained in this book.